FACES OF THE FREUDIAN "I"

FACES OF THE FREUDIAN "I"

The Structure of the Ego in Psychoanalysis

Mikkel Reher-Langberg

Routledge
Taylor & Francis Group

LONDON AND NEW YORK

First published 2018 by Karnac Books Ltd.

Published 2018 by Routledge
2 Park Square, Milton Park, Abingdon, Oxon OX14 4RN
711 Third Avenue, New York, NY10017, USA

Routledge is an imprint of the Taylor & Francis Group, an informa business

Copyright © 2018 by Mikkel Reher-Langberg

British Library Cataloguing in Publication Data

A C.I.P. for this book is available from the British Library

ISBN-13: 9781782205715 (pbk)

Typeset by V Publishing Solutions Pvt Ltd., Chennai, India

CONTENTS

ACKNOWLEDGEMENTS

I would like to thank Judy Gammelgaard and Andrew Moskowitz for their encouragement, critique, and confidence in me, without which I could not have undertaken the present study. I also wish to thank Jon Frederickson for his generous editorial suggestions, and for his writings, which stimulated my interest in the ego in the first place. Last but not least, I want to thank my friend Joachim Meier for our tireless discussions on subjectivity—a continual source of vitality and inspiration during the years of this book's conception.

ABOUT THE AUTHOR

Mikkel Reher-Langberg is a clinical psychologist based in Copenhagen, who works with a focus on intensive short-term dynamic psychotherapy and Lacanian psychoanalysis.

FOREWORD

The ego is one of the most well-defined and comprehensible psycho-analytic concepts, due in no small part to the long tradition of the school of ego psychology. Although it was there from the beginning of his work, for a long time Freud was occupied more with defining and qualifying the concept of the instinct than with its counterpoint the ego. It was not until the introduction of narcissism that Freud was forced to re-think his former, more loosely defined concept of the ego. The ego from the late period of Freud's thinking was the result of an evolution not only in the theory, but also in the subject of its investigation, a fact that does not surprise us, as this is a distinctive trait in the whole of Freud's theoretical work.

Reading Mikkel Reher-Langberg's book makes us realise that the concept of the ego, or *I* as the author has wisely chosen for Freud's *Ich*, is far more complicated than previously thought, and that it is a part of Freud's thinking throughout his work. This does not mean, however, that the *I* retained an identical function and position. On the contrary, the concept of the *I* does not follow a linear development in Freud's thinking, nor does it receive an unambiguous definition.

The point of departure and the aim of the present book are to inves-tigate the concept of the *I* throughout Freud's writing. Freud's thoughts are presented chronologically, focusing on those texts where Freud, for different reasons, seems to be forced to rethink the concept. One of the most interesting and original qualities of this book is that the author remains loyal to a central trait in Freud's thinking underlying its many contradictory perspectives, namely its characteristic paradoxicality and polyvalence, which Freud does not find it necessary to reconcile or synthesise. Another equally important strength is that although the pivotal concept is that of the *I*, the book can also be read as an introduction to Freud's *oeuvre* in general. Approaching Freud's work from the angle of the *I* reveals some quite new and sometimes rather surprising perspectives. This broadens the book's scope to reveal an eye-opening view of some of Freud's most important texts.

There is a thread running through all four chapters that says that the *I* cannot be seen from one perspective only. There are, as the title suggests, more faces of the *I*. One pair of perspectives singled out by the author is that of the dynamic and diachronic versus the structural and synchronic viewpoint. From the perspective of the *I* itself, it is defined as an agent of higher psychological functions, while forces or motives seem out of sight. From another perspective, in which the the *I* is viewed as a libidinal cathected object providing material for intrapsychic structure, the *I* as phenomenologically accessible appears rather as a "frozen image".

Starting from where Freud began, the first chapter takes us into *Studies on Hysteria* and its theoretical counterpart, *Project for a Scientific Psychology*. The hysterogenic mechanism, Breuer and Freud argued, was caused by a withholding or inhibition of a strongly felt impulse leading to a dissociation of the affect from its corresponding idea, implying an incompatibility in the psyche. The concept of the *I* was accordingly based on the observation of a conflict giving the impetus for resistance, defence, and repression, thus foreshadowing the idea of the unconscious. As an agent, the *I* appears as will, which is also often defined as counter-will against threatening impulses. In addition, the *I* can be characterised as an image or representation that stands in a special relation to a pathogenic core. At first, Freud called this a *foreign body* or *parasite*, but later changed to the term *infiltrate*. This term points towards the later model from *The Ego and the Id*, where the borders between conscious and unconscious are more blurred than the early model of conflict and repression suggest.

While *Studies* was based on clinical experiences, Freud was simultaneously engaged in complicated theoretical speculation on how to envisage the psychic apparatus in a scientific, neurological way. The dense and rich *Project for a Scientific Psychology* discloses a view of the *I* similar to the one presented in his clinical work. While being the locus of repression, reality-testing, attention, etc., the *I* can also be seen as a structurally defining entity in the psychic apparatus, bordering between primary and secondary processes.

Co-reading these two major works from the early days of psychoanalysis raises the question of what status should be attributed to Freud's neuropsychological model. The author wisely prefers to answer the question in a way that escapes the fallacy of both subjectivism and biology, viewing Freud's text as "a struggle to establish something beyond both" (p. 14). Summing up the readings of the two texts, this "beyond" can be seen as a way of mapping the dynamics of the psychic apparatus, and, in that way, creating a new object for a scientific investigation of neuroses. The internal psychic life is therefore not the nervous system itself, nor can it be reduced to mere psychology, as it operates by laws and forces beyond the conscious subject. It might also be said, and the author does, that the *I* is both the conscious subject itself and the totality of the psyche. This double illusion, as unfolded by Freud, means that the *I* creates its own unconscious shadow: "The *I*, then, is an object thought by itself to be an agent" (p. 17). It may be added that Freud's *Project* could be read as a scaffold serving the function of visualising a psychic apparatus, which might explain the psychological phenomena of neuroses. This scaffold collapses, however, with the recognition of its inborn limits.

What may we learn about the *I* by reading Freud's masterpiece *The Interpretation of Dreams*? Not a great deal it seems, as the work is, primarily, an investigation of the unconscious mechanisms of the dream-process. The *I* is still there, however, this time taking up a different position, which was hinted at in the *Project*, by establishing itself at the border between the latent and manifest levels of the dream. Thus, the *I* may be seen as an effect of the structuring processes of the unconscious and not simply as an opposing force to the unconscious.

The chapters on Freud's *Interpretations of Dreams, Narcissism*, and the *Ego and the Id* are the most complex and constitute the author's most important contribution to a re-investigation of the Freudian *I*. It is not possible for me to render the full complexity of ideas arising from these last chapters of the book. I must limit myself to highlighting what seem to be the most important ideas. One main question arising from investigating Freud's theory of the dream is whether the focus should be on the link between certain sets of inputs and the manifest result of the dream, or rather to focus on the dreamwork itself as "having a voice of its own beyond the representations it manipulates?" (p. 23). Favouring the latter, the next question concerns the relationship between unconscious processes and the *I*. It turns out that Freud's *Interpretation of Dreams* discloses quite a new perspective on the relationship between the unconscious and the *I*, raising the question of where we should place the *I* in the process of dreaming. The concept of the wish turns out to hold the key. The wish has a central role, as we know, and not only as a motivating force compared to repressed memories from *Studies*. The wish of the dream reveals, in fact, another idea of the unconscious as something inaccessible to consciousness, as in it is not capable of becoming conscious. The wish turns out to be more complex than the term suggests; it implies both a dynamic and a structural perspective. The wish, as is plain from Freud's term *Wunschregung*, is simultaneously an impulse and the realisation of its satisfaction.

In 1925, Freud found it necessary to add a footnote to his *Interpretations of Dreams* in order to make it clear that his focus had been on the dreamwork and not on the latent material calling for an interpretation. In short, the wish is embedded in the very process of making it manifest. Considering the role of the *I* and following Freud's assertion that wishes that are fulfilled in the dream "are invariably the ego's wishes", Reher-Langberg concludes that this must imply a continuity between the *I* and the unconscious. In other words, what we call repressed impulses arise "in an earlier state of the *I*" and "wishes of the *I* are implicitly directed 'around' those of the unconscious as 'structure'" (p. 34). Reher-Langberg raises an interesting subject, which may be formulated as a question: Could it be so that the continuity between the *I* and the unconscious implies that the *I* during the dream is situated as an invisible figure, partaking nonetheless in the primary processes of the dream? I read the following argumentation as affirming this.

Freud's *Interpretation of Dreams* has revealed a double perspective concerning the *I*. On the one hand, a dynamic perspective, defining the *I* in its function as censor struggling with the repressed, implying a reified, structurally primary *I*. On the other hand, the *I* of the dream-book is also deeply embedded in the transforming process of the wish. The *I* does not so much have a wish, but "is *embodying* a wish of another level of organisation" (p. 43).

On Narcissism: An Introduction is in many ways a remarkable and important turning point in the development of Freud's thinking, even though he subsequently left it in parentheses. Whereas earlier, the *I* was closely related to the conscious system, another face of the *I* is now revealed. Narcissism implies that the *I* no longer takes a contrasting position to the drive, but is itself an object of libidinal cathexis, thus signalling the collapse of the previous contrast between the two terms of ego and libido. Freud took the consequence and turned the dualism of sexuality and ego-instincts into that of Eros and the death-drive. As Laplanche (2002/2003) has expressed it, turning sexuality into Eros is not only a change of term, but also a transformation in the reality of a human being; a transformation from nature to culture, so to speak.

The many dilemmas contained in *On Narcissism: An Introduction*, such as primary narcissism and the corollary question of how the ego is developed alongside narcissism, have been answered differently by Freud's successors. One trend has been to dissolve the dilemmas by introducing the concept of the self as a cornerstone of narcissism, while others, on the contrary, have read Freud's introduction on narcissism in the perspective of his late drive dualism. Thus understood, primary narcissism illustrates how the ego takes part in structuring the satisfaction of the drive, either by keeping tension constant or by reducing it to zero. Opposing Freud's idea of the death drive, Green (2001) has pointed to the double face of narcissism containing both a negative or death narcissism striving towards zero or inertia, to use a term from the *Project*, and a positive narcissism striving towards unity and pleasure, while Laplanche (1999a) has chosen to speak of sexual life drive and sexual death drive.

Reher-Langberg's exposé of Freud's *On Narcissism: An Introduction* and its predecessors follows the tradition of the just-mentioned analysts. However, he approaches the drive from the point of view of the *I*, asking what lessons we may learn about the *I* as mediator of the drive. Once more we are presented with two different, albeit interwoven, stories of the *I*. The author has chosen Laplanche's differentiation between a *metonymical* and a *metaphoric* derivation of the *I* as guidelines for these two stories, which are unfolded inside the general frame of *I* in its relation to the drive.

The metonymic conception implies an *I* as a substantially displaced representative of what may be called the subject of the organism functioning as representative of the external world and defined through its ego-instincts. This is the *I* of adaptation and control, struggling to secure its own autonomy. With *On Narcissism: An Introduction*, another *I* is presented, which is adapted more to the desire of the other and represented in the psychic apparatus as object for itself. This is the metaphoric depiction of the *I*. Rather than being opposed to the drive, it is now depicted as partaking in the formally conceived aim of the drive. How shall we understand this? According to the author, it means that the *I* from the perspective of narcissism is an *I* of desire, marked in its centre by the imprint of the other and structured around the gaze of its internalised ideal.

Arguing against a reading of Freud's controversial concept of primal narcissism as a primal stage, Reher-Langberg dissolves the dilemma implied by the Freudian concept, arguing that primal narcissism is rather "a *fundamentally* lost perfection, functionally a *myth* of a 'pre-critical' oneness with the caregiver driving the circular movement through the ideal" (p. 63). We must accept that the paradoxical character of "a *narcissistic object* is necessary, since the *I* must logically find objects to imitate in order to attain the ideal" (ibid.).

Concerning the question of how the ego is developed out of the state of narcissism, Freud is not very precise when talking about a "new psychic action". Understanding the *I* as a metaphoric derivation from the subject, this new action may, however, be seen as a mirror-effect introducing a gap or difference, allowing the *I* to reflect upon itself as object. "As such, one is able to make sense of the paradoxical circularity of the subject coming into existence by falling in love with its own body, thus constituting the subject as its own object by becoming its own *other*" (p. 60).

1920 meant a radical turning point in Freud's theory, not only of the drive but also of the psychical apparatus, as well implying a revision of the ego's formal and dynamical aspects. The consequence of recognising unconscious processes within the ego has led many analysts to favour the idea taken from neuroscience of implicit memory at the cost of repression. This has had grave consequences not only for the idea of repression, but also for Freud's theory of the subject defined radically as de-centred. The author of this book proposes another reading of

Freud's late model, focusing on the structural and dynamic relationship between the *I* on the one hand and the id and superego on the other.

In the last chapter of the book, Reher-Langberg continues using the metonymic and metaphorical images of the *I*, arguing that now this doubling is found in the same place. The *I* is both a projection or displacement of a surface onto the body and the mirroring effect of the identification with the other. Furthermore, the *I* has lost some of its solidity while the boundaries between conscious and unconscious are blurred, as we see in the field of fantasy-formation, which to a large extent is unconscious. Concerning the internal relation between id, ego, and superego, it is argued that we have here a synchronic structure visualised in the unconscious fantasy, defined as a driving script, and a diachronic aspect, illustrative of the relationship between the *I* and the superego. The superego "now diachronically acts as a structure defining an intrapsychic libidinal circuit upholding a definition of the *I* within the bounds of the parental (paternal) ideal" (p. 79).

The structuring function of the superego is described as being "within a drive circuit with the *I*, so the id must be understood in a similar circuit with the *I*, this time defined by the concept of the *death drive*" (p. 79). This last circuit is illustrated clinically by negative narcissistic phenomena and by the tendency of the id to discharge independently of and incompatibly with the narcissistic structure, e.g., the *repetition compulsion*. In the two circuits described, the *I* is the defining centrepiece, mediating also the influence of libidinal energy on the organic sphere, whether in the form of law-abiding stability or symptomatic disruption.

Reading Reher-Langberg's tour de force through Freud's writing and re-writing of the *I* leaves an impression of the amazing complexity of the subject and Freud's continuous re-examination of it, as his ideas developed. Above all, however, this book tells the story of a core concept in psychoanalysis, recognising its characteristic ambiguity.

Judy Gammelgaard
Professor emerita, psychoanalyst, and
member of the International Psychoanalytical Association

INTRODUCTION

The aim of this book is to undertake a study of the notion of the *I* such as it evolves throughout the writings of Sigmund Freud. In publishing it, I have three hopes.

First, that shedding light on the psychic nature of man in Freud's thought, such as it will be argued to be encapsulated, even crystallised, in his notion of the *I*, is inherently relevant to the orientation of psychoanalytic thought and practice. A case will be made for this shortly.

Second, to my knowledge surprisingly few authors, with the notable exceptions of Mikkel Borch-Jacobsen and Jean Laplanche to whom I am greatly indebted, have undertaken the task of studying the evolution of the Freudian *I* in both breadth and depth. It is therefore my hope that presenting a chronologically broad yet philosophically precise survey of the *I* in Freud's work will contribute to filling out a lack in the literature, and that a presentation of this kind will be of interest also to those outside the clinical field.

Third, that the book will contribute to the dialogue between "psychodynamically" oriented and "post-structuralist" approaches to psychoanalytic thought within and without the clinic, which regrettably seem to have been severed in the wake of Lacan's critiques of especially American psychoanalytic traditions. Whereas the former are accused of reifying the *I* as an adaptive extension of the subject, ignoring the phantasmic basis of its being, the latter are accused of reducing the *I* to an imaginary epiphenomenon, neglecting its structuring function in intrapsychic dynamics and extrapsychic adaptation. As will be seen throughout the readings ahead, however, a central trait in Freud's thinking appears to be polyvalence, a paradoxical coexistence of apparently incompatible perspectives, without any sense of a necessary movement towards their synthesis or a prioritisation of either. Dynamic depictions of a reified, defensively active ego thrive unhindered among passages undermining both the substance and agency of such an ego, and this tendency is so consistent as to appear to be a central trait of Freud's theory as a whole. Rather than side with any of these schemes, then, it is my hope that a depiction of their equally constant presences will in itself act as a reason for ascribing their very coexistence an importance in an understanding of the truly Freudian vision of psychoanalysis.

Returning to this book's first aspiration, in order to grasp why the Freudian notion of the *I* could still be of importance to the orientation of psychoanalytic thought and practice today, a detour back in time might be helpful.

During the 1950s, French psychoanalyst Jacques Lacan emphatically argued how the adaptation of Sigmund Freud's originary psychoanalytic vision of man to different cultures and their norms had over time led to divergent readings of the Freudian *oeuvre*. This had in turn resulted in a global psychoanalytic movement held together by a heritage of words, shaping an illusion of unity among their users, while in actual practice confounded by divergent ideologies (Lacan, 1991, p. 11). Still today similar concerns are voiced about how "[P]sychoanalysis is a language rich in vocabulary but poor in grammar" (Fayek, 2013, p. 6).

Lacan, as many would come to do after him, therefore called for a "return to Freud" (1957) so as not to lose sight of the Freudian core of psychoanalysis, and in order to bring the practice of psychoanalysis back in accordance with its ethics. This return amounts to more than nostalgia or a need for dogma. Rather, it is a return to Freud's conception of man, orienting how such a man may and should be affected so as to facilitate change in his being. Reshaping psychoanalysis in accordance with the vision that spawned its vocabulary thus also reaches to the very core of psychoanalytic practice.

For Lacan and others following him, the term "subject" is often used to denominate the particular aspect of man with which Freud's revolution was concerned, and to which I shall attempt, vis-á-vis Lacan, to return in the following readings. But why ascribe such importance for a therapeutic praxis to something as seemingly philosophico-theoretical as "the subject"? Why concern oneself thoroughly with the abstract nature of the patient himself, or more specifically his subjectivity, that is his relation to himself, rather than the entities with which he struggles—the drives, phantasy, the unconscious?

Modern conceptions of subjectivity tend to approach the subject as a primarily epistemological entity (Mansfield, 2000). A certain view of the subject thus perceived essentially affords certain interactions, certain supposedly inherent possibilities and lines of development, a posteriori affirmed by the results of such interactions. In this way, the assumed internal mechanisms and potentials a specific conception of man imply act as a kind of lever by which, in the words of Nikolas Rose, "[P]sychology constitutes its object in the process of knowing it" (1998, p. 49). The subject one sees, then, is by definition the subject one acts on. In Freud's case, the core around which his psychoanalytic treatment developed can be argued to be exactly a novel view of the subject, as implied in his famous statement, heralding his very own Copernican revolution: *"daß das Ich nicht Herr sei in seinem eigenen Haus"* (G. W., 12, p. 10) ["that *the ego is not master in its own house"* (1921c, p. 143)].

Where is one to find this sense of man, this defining centre of Freudian subjectivity, in Freud's own works? In the most obvious place, I would argue, in the notion of the *Ich*, the *I*, since "In psycho-analysis ... we like to keep in contact with the popular mode of thinking and prefer to make its concepts scientifically serviceable rather than reject them" (1926e, p. 195). This word, "*I*", stands out as a point of continuous theoretical attention in Freud's work, developing as a centrepiece in his total theory of the psychic apparatus. As such, an approach to understanding the specifically Freudian vision of psychoanalysis through the conception of the *I* is arguably well in line with Freud's own thought. What is more, Freud's perhaps most famous formulation of the transformative potential of psychoanalytic practice is strictly tied to the concept of the *I*, resounding as a programme statement at the end of his thirty-first lecture: *"Wo Es war, soll Ich werden"* (G. W., 15, p. 86).

This is a paradoxical aim, however, when read along with the previous proclamation that the *I* is essentially not master in its own house. But perhaps, and as will indeed be argued, this paradox inherent to the Freudian *I*—between its essential dethroning and its status as central object of therapeutic concern—spells out with particular clarity a certain paradox in Freud's psychoanalysis as such, and thus further justifies its understanding by way of the nature of the *I*.

If the notion of a Freudian *I* sounds somewhat foreign, it may be due to the fact that subjectivity, throughout the history of psychoanalysis, has been closely tied rather to the notion of an *ego*, acting as a developmental epicentre—ontogenetically as well as in the history of the psychoanalytic movement itself. As put by Lacan:

> ... all subsequent development of analytic technique has revolved around the conception of the *ego*, and that is where we must locate the source of all the difficulties arising out of the theoretical elaboration on this development in practice. (1991, p. 15)

Translating the *I* as "ego" however, so far from everyday language, does not do full justice to Freud's insistence on conceptualising, through the use of his *Ich*, not so much an abstract entity separate from the phenomenological self, but the very "core" or *locus* of subjectivity in all its aforementioned complexity. As pointed out by Laplanche and Pontalis (1973, p. 131), the Freudian *I* spans exactly the vast range of *I*'s common sense implications, exploiting its traditional embeddedness in contrasts such as organism and environment, subject and object—but what is more, Freud plays on such ambiguities by blurring their boundaries.

Even a superficial reading of Freud's works reveals the complexity of his use of the word *Ich*. The central ambiguity is captured by Clifford Yorke (1994) when he argues that *Ich* is often not the executive representative of the requirements of reality that the *das Ich* of the structural model has been argued to be (Hartmann, 1939), but rather resembles what later analysts have called a "Self" (Phillips, 1988). Still, one is bound to agree with Laplanche and Pontalis when they point to how one must be careful not to reduce this complexity:

> ... it seems inadvisable to draw an outright distinction between the ego as the *person* and the ego as a psychical *agency*, for the very simple reason that the interplay between these two meanings is the core of the problematics of the ego. (1973, p. 131)

Coming to terms with the Freudian *I* then clearly requires an openness to complexity, perhaps even contradiction, and a central task in the following readings will be to delineate such complexity. It will be seen, as already indicated, how this turns out to be graspable as a curious double nature of the *I*, consistently and simultaneously depicted as what shall tentatively be called an "*I* as subject" and an "*I* as object". As will be argued, however, despite their intimate connection, any mistaking of the *I*, a meta*psychological* notion of a homunculus or image of sorts, structuring or defining the nature of subjectivity, for the subject proper, a meta*physical* notion with no place in the Freudian psyche as such, is an illusion inherent in the *I* itself which the reader must carefully avoid. However privileged its place with respect to subjectivity, the *I* must be understood as part of the *psyche*, rather than the subject per se (Butler, 1997), or perhaps as bridging these two realms.

Structure

As such, the present study of the Freudian *I* should also be able to serve as a textually broad yet thematically concise introduction to Freud's work in general. Luckily, with respect to the development of the *I* in Freud's work, there appears to be a wide consensus among scholars— however great disagreements arise from there—on where to draw lines between its phases (e.g., Hartmann, 1956; Køppe & Olsen, 1981; Lacan, 1988; McIntosh, 1986; Rothstein, 1981; also roughly following the three phases indicated in Jones, 1953):

1. First the *Studies on Hysteria* (1895d) and the *Entwurf* of 1895 (1950c), representing Freud's thought before,
2. the second phase initiated by *The Interpretation of Dreams* (1900a),
3. followed by the metapsychological works between 1905 and 1920 with "On Narcissism: An Introduction" (1914c) as the centrepiece,
4. and *The Ego and the Id* (1923b) introducing the structural model as a centrepiece of the period from *Beyond the Pleasure Principle* (1920g) and forth until Freud's last words in 1938.

To conclude then, the survey of the Freudian *I* presented in this book will focus on these few central works, read in their respective chronological contexts, and with a keen eye for contradiction. Furthermore, in order best to depict the chronological evolution of the *I*, the readings will be restricted to utilising notions in Freud's thought that are manifestly apparent in his works up until the time in question.

CHAPTER ONE

Studies and *Entwurf*: the apparatus of will

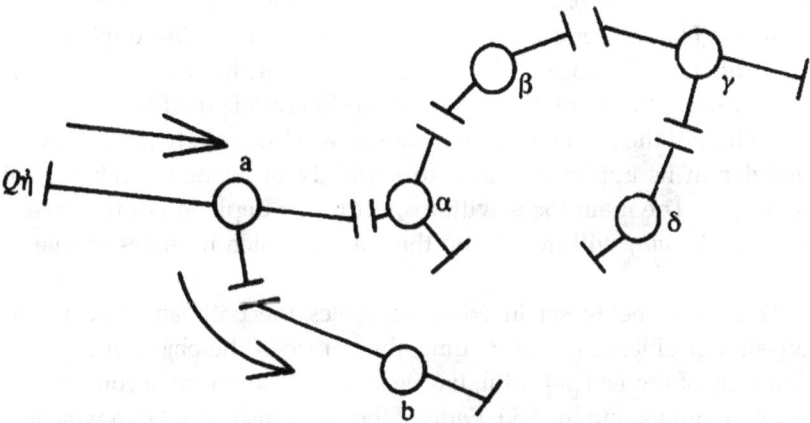

Figure 1. *The I—α-β-γ-δ ... —as a network of "neurones"* (Freud, 1950a, p. 324, illustration from Freud 1980, p. 67).

Preface

Our review of Freud's conception of the *I* takes its departure from two of Freud's earliest major works; the *Entwurf einer Psychologie* (henceforth *Entwurf*, the term meaning *draft* rather than the *S. E.*'s "project") and the *Studien über Hysterie* (henceforth *Studies*), as representing Freud's thought up until 1900. In order to grasp the specifically Freudian notion of the *I* at this point, the writings are furthermore contextualised by the ideational currents of the psychiatric environment that surrounded Freud during these early years.

Attention is initially and primarily paid to Freud's clinical works, since the phenomena described here supply the material and occasion for his theoretical elaboration of the "psychic apparatus" in general, and thus the *I* as a part of it. From this clinical basis, a "Freudian anthropology" depicting the moral predicament of the neurotic is deduced, by which the nature and function of the *I* as seen through the lens of pathology and treatment are allowed to stand out.

No review of Freud's writings of the 1890s, however, can ignore the *Entwurf*, the "Rosetta Stone" of psychoanalysis (Åge Haugland in Freud, 1980, p. 166). In this sketch, originally sent to and stored by Wilhelm Fliess, Freud engages in perhaps the most thorough depictions of the substance and function of the *I* in his entire *oeuvre*. As will be seen, however, the vision of the *I* herein is qualitatively similar to that of the aforementioned clinical works, though quantitatively broader in its application of it to a variety of normal-psychological functions. The main focus with respect to the depiction of the Freudian *I* in *Entwurf* will thus be on the way in which it relates to that of *Studies*.

Due to its being set in what resembles the pathoanatomical and physiological language of its time, the nature of the object of *Entwurf*, and thus of the *I* as part of it, has been subject to no small controversy since its publishing in 1950. *Entwurf* therefore also supplies a welcome occasion for discussing the ontological status of the Freudian *I* in general, which will be done at some length.

Studies on Hysteria: *a Freudian anthropology*

During the 1880s, the first written testimonies to Freud's preoccupation with hysterical phenomena start appearing. This preoccupation would come to form the material basis of Freud's general "anthropology", as well as his psychoanalytic cure. The phenomenon and its cause, however, had already been disputed for decades all across Europe. Before moving on to the *Studies*, then, a quick view across the scientific landscape in which they took shape and Freud's place in it seems necessary.

Pathogenic ideas

As argued by Kenneth Levin (1978), the central dispute structuring the scientific landscape in psychiatric circles by the time Freud arrives at the scene concerned the nature of hysteria. By major psychiatric thinkers of Freud's time, hysteria was firmly established as a pathoanatomical phenomenon, explained within a diathesis–stress model, in which a "neurotic predisposition" by itself, defined as degenerate heritage, tendency towards hypnoid states or otherwise, would render certain ideas, however meaningless, pathogenic.

Early on, though, one finds Freud firmly drawn to the more physiologically oriented Jean-Martin Charcot and his followers, viewing hysteria as being rather a functional illness. Furthermore, long before his decisive leap into purely psychological territory (e.g., 1900a, p. 536), one notes Freud's insistence on understanding neurotic phenomena by means of a strictly psychological vocabulary, often in stark contrast even to his physiologically minded contemporaries (Levin, 1978, p. 66). To draw forth just one example, in his encyclopaedia article on hysteria of 1888, Freud clearly states how:

> Hysteria is a neurosis in the strictest sense of the word—that is to say, not only have no perceptible changes in the nervous system been found in this illness, but it is not to be expected that any refinement of anatomical techniques would reveal any such changes. Hysteria is based wholly and entirely on physiological modifications of the nervous system. (1888b, p. 41)

Furthermore, with respect to its treatment , Freud continues on the same note:

> It is even more effective if we adopt a method first practised by Joseph Breuer in Vienna and lead the patient under hypnosis

> back to the *psychical prehistory* of the ailment and compel him to
> acknowledge the *psychical occasion* on which the disorder in ques-
> tion originated ... It is the method most appropriate to hysteria,
> because it precisely imitates the mechanism of the origin and pass-
> ing of these hysterical disorders. (ibid., p. 56, emphasis added)

One notes here Freud's insistence on hypnotic techniques as treating
the very *origins* of the illness. In an 1889 review of Auguste Forel's
"Hypnotisme", Freud goes even further in stating that:

> ... suggestion furthermore satisfies all the requirements of a causal
> treatment in a number of cases. This is so, for instance, in hysteri-
> cal disorders, which *are the direct result of a pathogenic idea* or the
> deposit of a shattering experience. If that idea is got rid of or that
> memory weakened—which is what suggestion brings about—
> the disorder too is usually overcome. (ibid., p. 100, emphasis
> added)

With his emphasis on psychological aspects of the aetiology of hysteria,
it will be seen how Freud from the late 1880s and onward radicalises a
strictly functional physiological model of the condition into something
quite different.

During the first half of the 1890s, Freud engaged in a theoretical
collaboration with the renowned Viennese physician Joseph Breuer, in
collaboration with whom he would come to write the aforementioned
Studies. In the book's co-authored *Preliminary Communication*, Freud
and Breuer argue that the hysterogenic mechanism is activated by the
withholding of an action upon a strong impulse (1895d, p. 1). This is
thought to lead to the "dissociation" of psychic excitation, or "affect",
from its representation, the psychic counterpart of the stimulus, causing the *idea* to become unconscious and the affect to displace itself by
strings of associations to other representations, most prominently of
the body, causing symptoms of conversion. By means of hypnosis, the
therapist accesses the pathogenic idea, inaccessible to normal recollection, and brings to an end

> ... the operative force of the idea which was not abreacted in the
> first instance, by allowing its strangulated affect to find a way

out through speech; and ... *subjects it to associative correction by introducing it into normal consciousness (under light hypnosis) or by removing it through the physician's suggestion, as is done in somnambulism accompanied by amnesia.* (ibid., p. 17)

Freud's radicalisation, however, concerns the reason for this withholding, and it is especially in contrast to the passages authored by Breuer alone that Freud's own views stand out.

Breuer depicts a psychic apparatus modelled on an electrical machine, its circuits progressively developed to pass endogenous and exogenous stimuli to expression (ibid., p. 183). The cause of psychopathology is conceived along similar mechanistic lines, in that the essence of psychic trauma is depicted as an overload of stimuli breaking the "insulation" of normal circuitry. This allows the current of information to spill over into other channels of expression, such as hallucinations and altered states of consciousness. The cause proposed is the sufferer having been in a vulnerable "hypnoid" state at the time of the trauma, the inclination to which is in turn ascribed to heritability. As such, the overload *by itself* is taken to be the trauma, hence the pathogenic "reminiscences" (ibid., p. 221) from which the patient suffers merely indicate the point of malfunction. Psychotherapy, then, lets trauma-related impulses be discharged by speech, an emergency circuit, in order simply to let the damaged one recover (ibid., p. 20).

By 1894, however, in his article on "The Neuro-Psychoses of Defence", no more than a year after writing the *Preliminary Communication* with Breuer, Freud's thought has arguably already taken a different turn. One now sees him focusing on the concept of *incompatibility—Unverträglichkeit* (G. W., I, p. 61), in turn depicted as giving rise to energetic short circuits through defences. Concurrently, as pointed out by James Strachey (Freud, 1894a, p. 46), the concept of the *I* ("ego" in the S. E.) appears twelve times in this short article, compared to zero times in the *Preliminary Communication*, since this is exactly the entity with which the affect is incompatible:

... *an occurrence of incompatibility took place in* [the hysterics'] *ideational life*—that is to say ... their ego was faced with an experience, an idea or a feeling which aroused such a distressing affect that the subject decided to forget about it. (Freud, 1894a, p. 47)

As a nucleus, such an idea now forms a *counter-will* exercising its impulses within the psychic apparatus, just like the one centred upon the *I*. As stated in Freud's "A Case of Successful Treatment by Hypnotism" of 1892–1893:

> The antithetic idea establishes itself, so to speak, as a *"counter-will"*, while the patient is aware with astonishment of having a will which is resolute but powerless … it may be that the antithetic idea is only able to put itself into effect because it is not inhibited by being combined with the intention. (p. 122)

The counter-will is, though, essentially tied to the will, the symptom to its carrier subject, since "… it is precisely through its repression that the idea becomes the cause of morbid symptoms" (1895d, p. 285).

As such, reminiscences are gradually emphasised as meaningful and thus pathogenic in and of themselves, exercising a continual pressure on the subject due to continual incompatibility in meaning. As expressed by Freud in "The Psychotherapy of Hysteria" in 1895:

> If I endeavoured to direct the patient's attention to [the idea], I became aware, in the form of *resistance*, of the same force as had shown itself in the form of *repulsion* when the symptom was generated. … Thus a psychical force, aversion on the part of the ego, had originally driven the pathogenic idea out of association and was now opposing its return to memory. The hysterical patient's "not knowing" was in fact a "not wanting to know". (ibid., p. 269)

By linking the aetiology as well as the mechanism of hysteria to the *I* and attempts at defence on its part, Freud could now engage directly with the illness in his attempts to defeat the resistances against spontaneous recollection of the pathogenic conflictual idea.

Far from a purely mechanic overload and passive splitting off, then, Freud now envisions a subject:

1. Actively exercising a *defence* and continual *resistance*—the hysterogenic mechanism,

2. towards an "idea"—the *material entity* or "nucleus" (1894a, p. 49) of the illness,

3. motivated by or growing from its *incompatibility* with the *I*—the actual cause.

Clinical implications

The move towards meaning is reflected in Freud's clinical works of the time. In the case of Emmy von N., dated by James Strachey to 1888 (1895d, p. 48), Freud speaks of his treatment as discharge of a residual sum of excitation by abreaction or thought-activity attained under hypnosis (ibid., p. 86)—much in line with Breuer's conception above. By 1892, in the case of Miss Lucy R. (ibid., p. 106), there is hardly any reference to hypnotic suggestion in Freud's technique—a trait now largely replaced by systematic recollection by associating freely and overcoming of the resistance encountered here. In the case of Fräulein Elisabeth von R., also of 1892, Freud speaks of the "strong resistance ... on the part of the patient's whole ego to come to terms with this ideational group", motivated by "great psychical pain", instead of which "physical pains made their appearance" by conversion (ibid., p. 166).

Freudian therapy can now even at this point be said to consist in convincing the subject to allow its associations to move towards the pathogenic idea, following the "logical chains" in which memories are assumed structured "concentrically round the pathogenic nucleus" (ibid., p. 289). The obstacle to such remembering, and thus the possibility of facing the pathogenic conflictual idea and so transforming "hysterical misery into common unhappiness" (p. 305), is essentially ascribed to "the subject's will" (p. 271), centred on the upholding of the *I*. The themes of the pain and resistance involved in recollection thus connect directly to the nature of the split-off ideas as defined by the *I*, establishing the effective cause of neurosis within structures of meaning. The resistance within certain ideational strands indicates as such not only sites of incompatibility, it also points to the themes of the very contents of the *I* that need to be modified in order to diminish such incompatibility.

It is furthermore interesting to note that such themes appear in Freud's cases to be structured by social contexts, defining the *I* equally in the eyes of others and of the subject itself. The upholding of the meaning of the *I* thus equals an upholding of certain socially defined positions: in the case of Elisabeth von R. (ibid., p. 135), a position defined by her father's wishes for her future, conflicting with her longing for a husband, or in the case of Miss Lucy (p. 106), that of a dignified servant and caregiver, incompatible with her love for the master of the house. Neurosis then essentially becomes a matter of "moral cowardice" (p. 123) with self-deception as a primary mechanism of retreat—a retreat essentially, as depicted in Freud's cases in *Studies*, from moral conflict, in order for the *I* to keep up appearances. In the words of Philip Rieff (1979, p. 308), then, neurosis is the penalty for ambition unprepared for sacrifice.

A Freudian anthropology

As such, the *I* is arguably the central culprit in Freud's early model of the aetiology of the neuroses, and the central object of therapeutic adjustment. It is now possible to take an informed look at the character of such an *I* as established in Freud's early clinical writings.

First of all, we encounter an *I* presented through its function as the centre of conscious will, though seemingly not equated with that. Its influence upon it is instead structuring, guiding, depicted as that of an ideal, an image, that is essentially an appearance to oneself and others. As such, it is the Archimedean point of conflict with whatever is incompatible with such an image. The *I* and the material with which the *I* is in conflict are, then, not qualitatively alien, but rather intimately related as reciprocally defined.

The *I*'s character of *image* rather than agent is further deepened in that the subject's will, perhaps best understood as the intentional direction of the organism, appears in Freud's anthropology to be decentred, revolving equally around certain "nuclei" of representations and around the *I*, which then in turn appears as just this: *a nucleus of preferred representations*. This now arguably establishes a bridge between the conscious subject and the *I*, in that the *I* represents the views of the subject within the psyche and vice versa, so that in order to consciously reach representations outside the *I*, the latter needs to bend its rigid character.

Just as the *I* structures the subject, then, the pathogenic idea structures the symptom. It is perhaps possible even to go as far as to view the *I* as the actual core of the symptom, evil twin of the subject, the logic of the pathogenic idea being essentially the same as that of the *I* in negative form. If the symptom is defined as a "compromise", as the pathogenic idea entering consciousness in a nonsensical form, cannot this too be said of the subject, caught between the eyes of society and the counter-will, centred on a representational nucleus, the *I*, structurally equal to the pathogenic one? Whereas Freud in his early writings speaks of the pathogenic idea as a "parasite" (1894a, p. 49), by 1895 one sees him turn against such a definition from the perspective of the *I*, inviting the reader to view it rather as an "infiltrate", indicating its continuity with the *I*, as a natural development of the logic of the psychic apparatus:

> A foreign body does not enter into any relation with the layers of tissue that surround it ... Our pathogenic psychical group, on the other hand, does not admit of being cleanly extirpated from the ego ... In analysis the boundary between the two is fixed purely conventionally ... In fact the pathogenic organization does not behave like a foreign body, but far more like an infiltrate. (1895d, p. 290)

The infiltrate, that which is strictly speaking foreign, is not the pathogenic idea by itself, but rather as Freud adds: "In this simile *the resistance* must be regarded as what is infiltrating" (ibid., p. 290, emphasis added)—a resistance thus substantiating the malignant bond between the *I* and its incompatible counterpart. In this way, it is not so much the incompatible idea as the incompatibility of such an idea that is foreign.

To conclude, the *I* at this point in Freud's writings appears defined by way of a paradox. In its insistence upon upholding a certain form, it reciprocally defines its own nemesis and establishes around such a counter-will, essentially confounding its illusion of freedom. In neurosis, every exertion of assumed freedom of the *I* is achieved through compromise (ibid., p. 192) and struggle with its own negative. The *I*, again paradoxically, can as such be read as the dynamic centre, not only of identity, but of deception as a means of self-control, its strength and prominence diminished proportionally to the force with which these are attempted to be exerted. Importantly also, the equation of the *I* as a rigid image with an exercising agent of the total psyche seems at this point in Freud's thought to be essentially the illusion of the *I*, blind to the decentred distribution of control within the psyche and unknowing of the nemesis necessitated by such hubris. Whereas the *I* insists on being its own subject, Freud in his early writings simultaneously banishes it to the place of an *object*.

Entwurf—a project for what science?

Such is the contour of the *I* in Freud's clinical works until 1895, the year in which *Entwurf* was written down during the month of September (1950a, p. 285). The stage is set and the expectations raised for this dense and lengthy theoretical work to take the place of a final proposition, a beginning or an end for the science of the unconscious and its workings that Freud had laid the ground for. It was, however, soon abandoned (Jones, 1953) or at least left behind (Kanzer, 1973) by Freud, never to be published in his lifetime—though from such a seemingly repressed position, as Strachey points out, and as will be apparent in the chapters to come, "… the Project, or rather its invisible ghost, haunts the whole series of Freud's theoretical writings to the very end" (Freud, 1950a, p. 290). The following exposition will begin by sketching out the nature of the concept of the *I* in this work, in order to then move on to consider the scientific and ontological status of the very substance such *I* is set in.

The I of Entwurf

In *Entwurf*, Freud envisions a psychic apparatus modelled on two basic tenets from which the entire text can be said to derive (Gill & Pribram, 1976): the *neuron doctrine* stating that such an apparatus is made up of interconnected structurally identical entities, and the principle of *Trägheit*, inertia, stating that such entities will attempt to reflexively discharge any and all energy with which they are "cathected", *besetzt*.

In order to survive and adapt, however, stable structures of discharge for endogenously generated excitation need to be developed, and as such a further distinction is proposed: a purely topological differentiation (Wilson, 1996, p. 30) into *memory* neurones "ψ", defined by having mutable barriers to connections, making learning by experience and organisation as such possible and thus making up the very body of the psyche, and *sensory* neurones "φ" with permeable barriers. In themselves, these both exist beyond consciousness, as the latter is said to reside in a third class of "ω" neurones.

The psyche as ψ, then, is an apparatus of *discharge by association*, and as such, one must distinguish between two kinds of discharge-processes: what Freud calls "primary" and "secondary" *Vorgänge* (*S. E.* reads "process[es]"—however, "proceeding" may be more precise).

These are defined respectively as the unobstructed mechanical passing of excitation among neurones, following the *Bahnungen* (*S. E.* reads "facilitation", but *Bahnung* carries with it notions of pathbreaking, *Bahn* translating as "track") established by experience, and by discharge affected by a core of stably cathected neurones in ψ, *the I*. Since no organism can be thought to subsist in a state of spontaneous discharge (see Freud, 1911b, p. 214), one may rather understand these as distinct types of intentionality driving any psychical movement towards pleasure and satisfaction respectively (Hill, 1980, p. 179).

The psychic apparatus thus operates according to two basic principles: the principle of *inertia*, accounting for a fundamental tendency towards spontaneous mechanical discharge, and a necessary principle of *constancy* by which the apparatus at a higher, emergent level of organisation keeps up an equilibrium of excitation.

From the operation of these two principles, two more of a seemingly different order are deduced: first, constancy is said to be upheld by actually effective discharges, logically implying a third *reality* principle, that is a distinguishing of actual from hallucinatory gratification. Second, although primary and secondary processes seem antagonistic, their underlying motivational force is the same, in assuming that any rise in excitation equals systemic tension and a "need" for discharge, qualitatively identifiable as unpleasure, implying a fourth *unpleasure principle* operant in the apparatus. Constancy, like inertia, essentially serves the function of discharge by, however paradoxically, upholding a certain tension, an *I*, as a lesser evil than the one faced by a system with no means of effectively satisfying its needs. The reader may already sense how these principles appear to mirror the neurotic conflict depicted in Freud's clinical works: pathogenic tension is produced as incompatible unconscious excitations approach the *I*, resulting in spontaneous discharge around the stable ideational core of the *I*, and thus without regard for actual gratification.

With the above in mind, the *I* one sees arise in Freud's early clinical writings arguably finds its general continuation in *Entwurf*, established on the level on which it presented itself in Freud's clinical experience. Though widely similar in character, Freud's interest in the *I* in *Entwurf* seems more comprehensive than in *Studies*. Rather than exploring certain clinical tendencies, Freud steps back and envisions a psychic apparatus as it might look if built upon the logic of such. The perspective, then, is at the same time equivalent and reversed:

> The problem he was attempting to solve was not simply how does
> the ego lose its nerve—or as he says, its moral courage—but how
> does it find it in the first place, (Hill, 1980, p. 182)

First of all, the *I* is defined as a stable ideational core within an otherwise
homogeneous network of representations (Freud, 1950a, p. 323). Its function is explicitly the *stören* of "Aufläufe ... die sich zum ersten Mal in bes-
timmter Weise ... vollzogen haben"[1] (1950c, *G. W., Nachtragsband*, p. 416)
following spontaneous ideational association. As with the structural reciprocity between the *I* and the symptom in *Studies*, this *stören* (interfering)
follows mechanically from the very nature of the *I*. Subject to inertia, the
I is driven to discharge its constant tension, and must do so by *overdetermining* arising needs in the organism, thus drawing energy away from
alternative associations to those within the *I* (1950a, p. 323).

Furthermore, since the neurons of the *I* are constantly cathected, their
Bahnungen are particularly open, lending relatively free passage to arising excitation. We see here the defensive function of the *I* raised from
a form of pathogenic cowardice to a universal principle of control and
organisation within the psychic apparatus, further stressing its derived
and mechanical character. Whereas in *Studies* the defence actualised a
border between will and counter-will, in *Entwurf* it embodies the point
of influence between primary and secondary processes.

As locus of the constancy principle and basis of the secondary process in general (1950a, p. 327), the *I* of *Entwurf* can, as in *Studies*, be seen
as the structurally defining entity in the psychic apparatus. As such, the
I again becomes the necessary point of emergence for a variety of functions—ascription of reality (ibid., p. 326), directional thinking (p. 329),
attention (p. 361), etc.—without ever being depicted as its actual agent.
Also, for instance, *will* is defined as the very passage of excitational discharge, irrespective of what drives it (p. 337).

As in *Studies*, the *I* is also the natural locus of repression, here defined
as the exclusion of certain ideas from the proceeding of thoughts, as
drawn towards habitual patterns. Hysteric compulsion, the "counter-
will" of *Studies*, results when entire *Vorgänge* are cut off from the
I-complex, and are driven to expression by the primary process alone,
following associations towards motor-representations irrespective of
their effects in reality.

As pointed out by Jean Laplanche (1987), the *I* must as such be conceived of essentially in its function of keeping "internal reality" at bay,

in order to lead excitation towards satisfaction in outer reality—all the while deriving its raison d'être and its very energy from primary "desires" for a specific form of discharge arising from such internal reality. As ironically pointed out by Melvyn Hill (1980, p. 176):

> In the end, the ego's capacity for effective action arises first, from the storehouse of memories of satisfaction that turn into wishes for satisfaction when freshly cathected, and second, from its ability to inhibit the cathexis of painful memories before they are aroused.

One sees in all this the image of an *I* as essentially a *slave of the passions*. Perhaps one might even propose, that whereas the "will" in *Studies* is established in the *I*, with *Entwurf* the *I* is rather defined as a "counter-will" to ontogenetically primary desires outside it, deriving its energy from such by inhibition. The strength of the *I* with respect to its functions consists in its ability to effectively satisfy the desires it is meant to administer. Compared to *Studies*, then, in *Entwurf* the reciprocity between the *I* and the ideas it antagonises is further developed.

Entwurf, a beginning

Even though the object of *Entwurf* is as such arguably well in line with that of *Studies*, it should be apparent from the above how *Entwurf* is cast in a language radically different from that of Freud's other works of the period. Whereas the latter operate on a level of socio-subjective meanings, intentions, and desires, *Entwurf* maps the psyche in purely mechanistic terms: as forces, connections, and assemblages, set in a quasi-neural space tentatively linked to the human brain (1950a, p. 303). This begs the question of how one is to interpret the metapsychological language that Freud uses in *Entwurf*, and thus what light it sheds on his findings in *Studies*. Is *Entwurf* "a 'neurological document', philosophically oriented, or a set of neurologically clad psychological propositions drawn from clinical observation and inductively developed" (Kanzer, 1973, p. 90)? Is Freud at this point a philosopher at heart, speaking the language of neurology (Lothane, 1998) or a natural scientist, expanding into philosophical territory (Gill & Pribram, 1976)? In order to be able to connect the notion of the *I* of *Entwurf* to Freud's thought in general, it is necessary to examine the text's formal characteristics and their implications for the scientific status of Freud's metapsychological constructions of which the *I* is one.

Critics of Freudian metapsychology have been known to make of this an occasion on which a purportedly mechanistic and reductive essence of Freud's science shows its true face, modelled on the biomedical, existentially estranging discourse of Freud's neurological heritage (Schafer, 1976; Wilson, 1996). Another reading of *Entwurf* as the last word of a pre-psychoanalytic quasi-neuroscientific phase soon to be disavowed is indeed a common one, even within orthodox psychoanalysis. However, as stated by Mark Kanzer (1973; see Borch-Jacobsen & Shamdasani, 2012 for elaboration), this conception may be widespread mainly due to its place in classical works such as the *Standard Edition* (e.g., 1950a, p. 290) and Ernest Jones's biography (1953).

Others make of it rather the essential *first* word of the establishment of a radically new science, one whose object is not to be found in the sphere of the psychological, the biological, or the social. According to Niels Egebak (1980), it is important to note how Freud consistently attempts to establish psychoanalysis on the *pattern* of a natural science, without explicitly aspiring to render psychoanalysis a *natural* science per se. Throughout his writings, Freud repeatedly stresses the point that the borrowed languages in which his theory is set merely scaffold an essentially invisible object, but must not be mistaken for it (ibid., p. 15). Rather than attempting to establish *Entwurf* on either side of an antagonism between subjectivism and biology that its object appears to defy, it appears fruitful to take a third way, viewing such ambiguity as the expression of a struggle to establish something beyond both.

On the basis of their seemingly qualitatively similar anthropological essences, one may take *Studies* and *Entwurf* to be two sides of one coin, both attempting to map the dynamics of the *psychic apparatus* as the new object of a science of the neuroses. The intrapsychic sphere, as we have seen, is not in itself the nervous system nor its impulses, since it is said only to reside functionally herein as an organisation. Neither is it psychological, since it reveals itself exactly as ideas slip beyond the reach of psychological explanation, operating by laws and forces beyond the conscious subject. Nor is it an aspect of social relations, since these appear to supply the structures with which the subject in illness finds itself unable to comply. It would thus appear that the Freudian intrapsyche must be located in a kind of gap between the affective organism with its arising needs and the conscious psychological subject, without being reducible to any of these.

The Freudian object

What then is the nature and substance of the object Freud circles around in his works up until 1895?

As pointed out by Niels Egebak (1980), the *nature* of such object is apparent in Freud's naming of it in *Entwurf*: a *psychic apparatus*, or *seelische Apparat*, soul-apparatus—a machine of sorts in which subjectivity, the soul, is necessarily embedded, even produced, yet out of sight, and never simply equalling this subjectivity, anthropologically defined by its lack of knowledge of its own overdetermination. It is a paradoxical object, then, embodying the very will of the subject, an *apparatus of will*, the movements of which are causally determined by laws and principles not apparent on the level of subjective experience.

In *Entwurf*, the *substance* of such an apparatus is described in terms of *neurons*, conceived essentially as a pure, empty network. As pointed out by Elizabeth Wilson:

> Having no biological essence, the neuron is unable to carry the origin of the psyche. This responsibility is displaced onto excitations, or more specifically the difference between excitations. (1996, p. 30)

Excitations, traces, movements, all set between essentially *ideational* points. Mark Kanzer further develops this thought in stating that:

> Freud's "neurones" and the processes among them were hypothesized not from actual observations in neurology ... but from clinical data, and they were used to explain clinical data, not to explain neurological data. Freud's "neurones" are in fact inventions: they are "psychical processes" which are to be *represented* "as quantitatively determined states of specifiable material particles". (1973, p. 91)

Readers of Freud tend to stress his thermodynamic heritage in the way he depicts the psychic apparatus as a kind of steam engine, transforming pressures and allocating them along one way when another is blocked

(Johnston, 2008). But it seems that in *Entwurf*, consistent with his earlier theorising, Freud also tends to regard it as an *information machine* (Gill & Pribram, 1976). As stated by Jacques Lacan, what one then sees firmly stressed even in this, Freud's most biological of metaphors, is the *symbolic* function of the psychic apparatus as a meaning-machine (Lacan, 1988, p. 76).

Conclusively, it can now be argued that what Freud does in *Entwurf* is essentially to strengthen his view of the psychic apparatus as defined not by autonomous entities or agents, but by organisations of ideas, the dynamics of which are tied to certain clinical phenomena. As such, the *I* now appears to be essentially a hypothetical topological locality incorporating certain ideas, and thus inevitably distancing others. Its *substance* is nothing more than such ideas, its *functions* the dynamic consequences of the systemic organisation it establishes.

Conclusion: approaching the Freudian I

The examined works until 1900 have now turned out to depict an *I* as a strictly metapsychological entity within a psychical apparatus, located in a hypothetical space between the organism and subjectivity. It is defined topologically as a group of prevalent ideas within a greater ideational network, establishing certain "secondary" processes of expression around it. It appears linked as a representative to the subject, and is the centre of intrapsychic dynamics, such as repression, resulting mechanically from the substantive definition of the *I*—a definition that is woven into social structures. Finally, such definition appears linked to social structures.

Functionally, the *I* is primarily defined by its role in psychopathology as the dynamic centre of incompatibility, rendering certain ideas pathogenic in excluding them from secondary processes, and thus allowing them free passage to symptomatic expression. Such exclusion considered as an act is the defence or resistance, appearing as a border-phenomenon whenever incompatible ideas "approach" the *I*, and whereby unpleasurable tension arising in such meeting is allowed to recede in ways short-circuiting the path through the *I*. This "dynamic" perspective on the psychic apparatus seems on one side aligned with that of the *I* itself, as implying a reified *I* in opposition to or complicit with its unconscious counterpart, but either way excluding a third term potentially confounding the substantiality of the *I*. On the other side, however, and as shall be elaborated on in the chapters to come, another perspective is hinted at in the way such "dynamic" perspective implies a misrecognition of the nature of the conflict it depicts, and one so fundamental as to perhaps be its very basis.

In *Entwurf*, Freud elaborates his definition of the *I* on a machinic level, without reducing the subject to non-subjective forces acting upon it—that is, without reducing subjectivity in itself to the scientific objectivity of a machine, such as he has been accused of (Gill & Holtzman, 1976). The *I* of *Entwurf* is not the conscious subject—it simply cannot be since this would imply its substantiation, and a theorisation from the point of view of the very subject that his discoveries are meant to shed light on. It appears though, that the Freudian *I* is here indeed a sort of stand-in for the subject, as the point of view from which he misrecognises himself, a point of necessary attachment that the subject is not able to see through or beyond, within a greater psychic structure. As such, this connection by its very nature embodies the double illusion essential to Freud's thought unfolded until now: that the *I* is the willing, conscious subject itself, and that the *I* is the totality of the psyche. Such blindness mirrors the paradoxical complicity of the *I* in its own hardship, as logically defining its own unconscious shadow with which it struggles. The *I*, then, is an object thought by itself to be an agent.

Note

1. "interferes with passages [of quantity] which on the first occasion occurred in a particular way" (1950a, p. 323).

CHAPTER TWO

The Interpretation of Dreams: the *I* decomposed

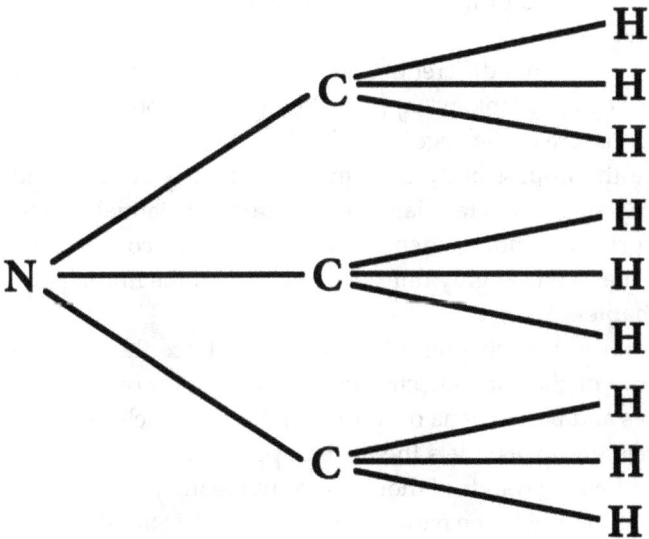

Figure 2. Chemical formula for trimethylamine exemplifying the structural overdetermination of the I in the unconscious wish.

Preface

From being the immediate object of primary concern in *Studies* and *Entwurf*, the *I* as a dynamically explanatory concept appears to shrink from centre stage in *The Interpretation of Dreams* (1900a) (henceforth *Dreams*).

Certain authors, perhaps most prominently Anna Freud (1936; see also Hartmann, 1956), have taken this as an occasion for letting *Dreams* demark the beginning of a Freudian "id psychology". Such a phase, characterised by neglect of preoccupation with as shallow a realm as that of the *I*, is said to reign in psychoanalysis until the structural model of the 1920s revives the concept (A. Freud, 1936).

Indeed, the *Standard Edition* rendering of *Dreams*, in many senses a rather voluminous work, uses the translation "ego" only forty-nine times, according to my count, and largely in the form of a theoretically vague attribute—"egoistical", rendered *"egoistisch"* in the original German (*G. W.*, 2). The *Standard Edition* texts of other major works of the same period—*The Psychopathology of Everyday Life* (1901b) and *Jokes and Their Relation to the Unconscious* (1905c)—show the same pattern, utilising the term "ego" only five and four times, respectively.

However, such a differentiation between an "id psychology" and a separate "ego psychology" appears to rely on the possibility of dissociating the nature of the "ego" from that of the "id"—and paradoxically so, since the impossibility of doing so is exactly Anna Freud's point (1936). As such, the Freudian *I* is rendered substantially autonomous and in principle independent of its unconscious counterpart—a conception that seems highly unfeasible in view of the findings of our previous chapter.

The aim in this chapter, then, will be to trace the development of the nature of the *I* as reflected in the elaboration of the unconscious processes and phenomena of concern in *Dreams*. Such an approach will prove rewarding, as it lets the reader appreciate what will be taken to be two different strands of thought simultaneously present in the book, and subsequently in the nature of the *I* in it.

The central concern in the ensuing discussion can be summarised in a question asked, and of course simply left hanging in the air as food for thought, by Jacques Lacan in his seminar of 1954:

> In the analysis of resistances do we have the equivalent of what we
> call the analysis of material? Is working on the procedures of the
> ego, or exploring the unconscious, of the same order? Are the two
> systems complementary? Are they the same with a change of sign,
> just about that? (1988, p. 59)

The answer will be that a yes and a no coexist within *Dreams*. Whereas
the *I* and the repressed in *Studies* and *Entwurf* were largely "the
same with a change of sign", the unconscious nucleus resembling a
Hegelian negative of the *I*, a different picture now tentatively arises.
While the unconscious in *Studies* served as an explanatory entity
edged in between organism and consciousness, in *Dreams* one sees it
established rather between the so-called latent and manifest dream
material rendering the unconscious a structuring function *enveloping* the *I* rather than simply opposing it on its own "level". Such a
move is made in an ambiguous, transitional manner, mirrored, as
will be seen, in a peculiar double nature of several central concepts
of *Dreams*—in this chapter especially those of censorship, the wish,
the unconscious, and identification. In order properly to capture such
ambiguity of the *I* of *Dreams*, a somewhat thorough discussion of the
nature of the dream as the phenomenon in which the *I* is here defined
must necessarily be undertaken, and it is to this task that we shall
first turn.

The dream and its place in the psychic apparatus

Freud's dream

As psychoanalytic orthodoxy rather tendentiously has it (Anzieu,
1987), Freud's definitive interest in dreams struck him as suddenly as,
on July 24, 1885, the nature of dreams was miraculously revealed to him
in a dream—the dream of Irma's injection to be discussed later—while
ruminating in his self-analysis on his father's recent death. A revela-
tion such that Freud would still, almost five years later, half-jokingly
fantasise of how a plaque would come to adorn the site of annuncia-
tion (1954, p. 323). Only a few months after this, he would elaborate at
length on that nature of dreams in *Entwurf*.

It is surely legitimate to criticise this account as yet another example
of the psychoanalytic community's self-verification through the writing

of its own history (Borch-Jacobsen & Shamdasani, 2012). However, one cannot but agree with Ernest Jones when he depicts the contrast between *Dreams* and the chapters on dreams in *Entwurf* as that between a mansion and a cottage (1953, p. 354). In both works, the dream is essentially *the fulfilment of a wish* (1950a, p. 340 and 1900a, p. 122). In *Entwurf*, however, the nature of the wish is plainly that of a rather immediate hallucinatory release of representational cathexis, vis-á-vis the primary process, fully in line with its general scheme of charge and discharge. In *Dreams*, on the other hand, the relation is the opposite: the dream as a phenomenon is here of primary concern, and as such it takes the driver's seat of theoretical development, from where it in turn is the one to put the psychic apparatus of Freud's earlier writings in line. All the while Freud, now better likened to the censor of a dream than its master, tries from the sideline to fit such heterogeneous struggling forces, the unruly reality of the dream and the mechanic schematics of the psychic apparatus, into one neat picture.

The following exposition of the nature of the *I* in *Dreams* shall begin, so to speak, at the manifest surface, the chapter written lastly but placed at the beginning of the book (Welsh, 1994, p. 5). Next, attention will be paid to the "latent" theory *Dreams* expresses, that of the concluding metatheoretical chapter 7 in which Freud assembles his theory of the nature of the dream from the hints scattered all over the preceding six chapters.

The decentred dreamer

Authors commenting on *Dreams* tend to hurry past its first chapter, in which Freud traces the history of dream interpretation until his present, as if it were merely an excessively long formality leading up to the actual substance of the book. I would argue, however, that as finished last but placed first, the chapter contains an essential message in enveloping and situating this content as a whole. Advertently or not, Freud in this long exposition retroactively establishes his own science of dreams as filling out a hole inherent in earlier theories, lending it the shine of a necessary development. In doing so, he denotes exactly the level on which the dream is to be located in his own theory of the psychic apparatus.

Such a level is demarcated in a way similar to that of *Studies* and *Entwurf* where Freud's fundamental question was in the nature of *"What mediates and thus determines the form of expression of the organic in the subjective?"* That is, what lies *between* the affects, the endogenous energies or stimuli, and the overly strong idea, the symptom? For Freud's antecedents, it has been clear that the dream expressed some idea or stimulus by means of another, and the key to the dream was to discover the former in the latter. It is, however, in this virtual space *between* such input and output, that Freud will once again establish his primary object of concern.

This time though, Freud adds a new dimension of abstraction to his inquiry, as both input and output are explicitly of a *psychical* nature, since the common view of the dreams as "but a somatic process signalising its occurrence by indications registered in the mental apparatus" leaves "no room for any problem of interpreting them" (1900a, p. 96). Rather, he proposes that certain "latent" *thought*-material, essentially memories or pieces of it, are by way of the unconscious "dreamwork" led to a "manifest" experiential expression, thus logically detaching the functioning of the mediating apparatus from the outside world as well as the organic body. As will be elaborated in the following, such a transposition now raises another question, namely between which set of inputs and outputs is the meaning of the dream to be found? Between the original sensational stimuli of the preceding day and the manifest "acts" of the dream, harking back to *Studies*? Or, somewhat further submerged in the medium of the unconscious, between the associations to such stimuli and the manifest dream-text, pointing rather towards the dreamwork as having a voice of its own beyond the representations it manipulates?

How to have a dream

In this vein, Jean Laplanche (2007, p. 177) clarifies how Freud in *Dreams* defines dream-production, like any other production of the unconscious, be it a symptom or a slip of the tongue, as a loop around stimulation and motility—"At the entry and at the exit, there are nothing but material actions" (ibid., p. 184):

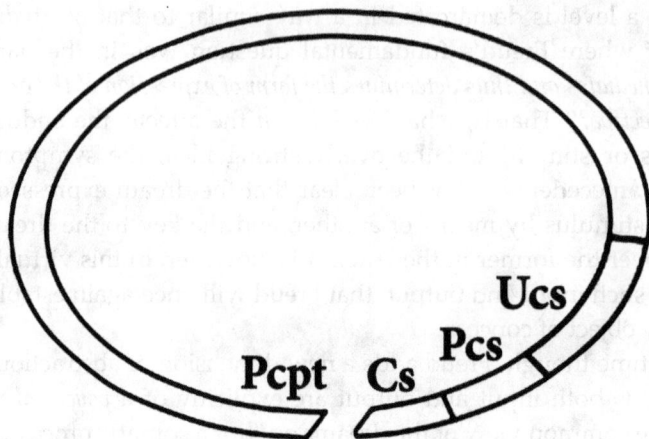

Figure 3. Freud's model of unconscious surgings up (illustration based on Laplanche, 2007, p. 191).

On both ends of the central gap, the point of contact of the psyche with the world, Freud locates two equivalent functions: perception, directed outward (*Pcpt.*) and inward as consciousness (*Cs.*), established however as separate locales driven by specific processes, much as in *Entwurf*. Mediating *Pcpt.* and *Cs.* on the inside of the loop, we find two locales: *Pcs.* "containing" psychical material dynamically available to consciousness, and *Ucs.*, simply "containing" the rest.

This seems to be a rather reduced model of the psychic apparatus, and indeed, as Freud himself points out (1900a, p. 537), the structural content of the model is *topographical*. This means that the model essentially depicts *a necessary order of progression* of intrapsychic stimuli or tensions, the stations of which are defined by "processes of excitation or modes of its discharge" (ibid., p. 610)—the familiar primary (*Ucs.*) and secondary (*Pcs.*) processes. As Laplanche notes, this is then not strictly a model of the mind in general, but rather one of "the surging up of what one might call, after Lacan, the 'formations of the unconscious'" (2007, p. 192). Such surgings up are now in general defined by Freud as *wishes*:

A current of this kind in the apparatus, starting from unpleasure and aiming at pleasure, we have termed a "wish"; and we have asserted that only a wish is able to set the apparatus in motion and that the course of the excitation in it is automatically regulated by feelings of pleasure and unpleasure. The first wishing seems to have been a hallucinatory cathecting of the memory of satisfaction. (1900a, p. 598)

Freud furthermore lets us know that the *Anstoß* (G. W., 2, p. 546)—a push, an instigation, but also an offence—to the construction of a dream stems from *Ucs.*: "[W]herever a dream has undergone distortion the wish has arisen from the unconscious" (1900a, p. 552). As this is always the case (except for some infantile dreams), Freud can conclude that "[A] dream is a (disguised) fulfilment of a (suppressed or repressed) wish" (ibid., p. 160). From here, it follows largely the same schema as in *Entwurf*: impulses deriving from unconscious representations reflectively tend towards discharge through conscious motility (p. 533).

During sleep, however, access from *Pcs.* to *Cs.* is closed off, and the impulse is forced to "regress" back through *Ucs.*, translating it once again into the primary process-driven patterns of organisation by sensorial contiguity dominant here, in order to then find expression in perception: "We call it 'regression' when in a dream an idea is turned back into the sensory image from which it was originally derived" (ibid., p. 543). This at the same time activates *Cs.*, since *P.* and *Cs.* are, as noted, essentially one system (ibid., p. 541, n. 1). *Cs.* is now confronted with a genuine re-imagined perceptual scenery, and from here a "secondary revision" sets in, in which the conscious subject selectively experiences the otherwise objectively manifest and rich dream-scenario, as it would its waking world.

The manifest dream is as such thought to be analysable into its constituent "latent dream-thoughts", which are simply the heterogeneous activated thought-material out of which it was composed, by following trains of associations back from each part of the experienced dream—just as with the symptoms in *Studies*. The whole process can be illustrated thus:

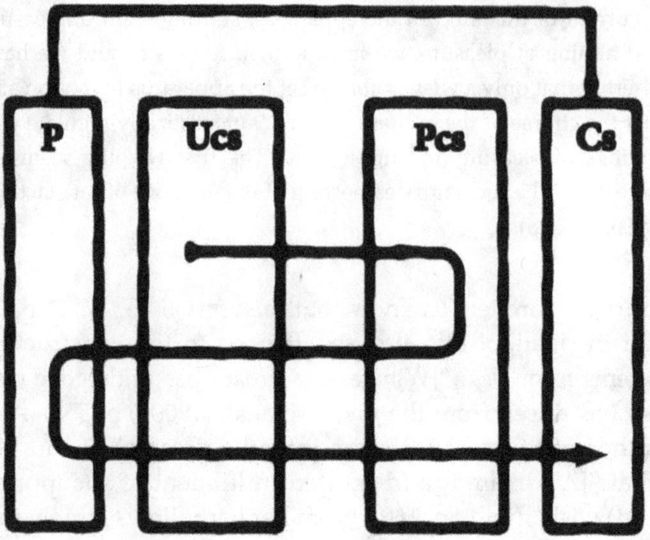

Figure 4.   The regressive movement of the Ucs. wish. Illustration after Køppe & Olsen (1981, p. 164).

The art of censorship

As in *Entwurf*, the movement between *Ucs.* and *Pcs.* implies a transformation, now essentially by *translation* between imagistic (*Ucs.*) and conceptual (*Pcs.*) form:

> The dream-thoughts and the dream-content are presented to us like two versions of the same subject-matter in two different languages. Or, more properly, the dream-content seems like a transcript of the dream-thoughts into another mode of expression. (Freud, 1900a, p. 277)

Simultaneously this "dreamwork" is understood as an intentional distortion: "The fact that the phenomena of [literary] censorship and of dream-distortion correspond down to their smallest details justifies us in presuming that they are similarly determined" (ibid., p. 143). By extension, the dreamwork is thought to satisfy not only the censorship (to be likened to the question of "compatibility" with the *I* in Freud's earlier works) and the wish to sleep undisturbed by troubling unconscious thoughts, but also in a purely mechanical way the very material striving for manifest form (Køppe & Olsen, 1981, p. 169).

Is the formation of the dream determined, then, by the unconscious itself or the *I*? In the previous works, the reasoning of the *I* could be said to reach to the core of the repressed unconscious, forcing its turn to primary process-development. Now, a "reasoning" of the unconscious seems to intersect rather with that of the *I* in the phenomenon of the dream, making it difficult to establish either one as primary.

In the *Standard Edition* (1900a, p. 615) it is further stated that the *Ucs.* is "inadmissible to consciousness". Such a translation seems to imply a definite and unpleasurable character of the "contents" of the *Ucs.*, harking back to the incompatibility of *Studies*. The original German, however, reads *bewußtseinsunfähig* (*G. W.*, 2, p. 619) implying, I would argue, simultaneously lacking acceptability and lacking *capability*, and thus, rather than mere overdetermination, two separate notions of the unconscious: initially the unconscious as repressed latent representational material—but also as something in itself unrepresentable. As constitutionally *unfähig* for representation, such unconscious "subject matter" only shows itself by cathecting what must now be understood as *Pcs.* representations, finding itself implied in their very organisation by the unconscious processes of dreamwork.

The discussion of *Dreams* so far indicates the tentative emergence of a new perspective on the relation between the *I* and the unconscious. The nature of such a perspective, though, is still at this point rather obscure, as are its antecedents in Freud's thought. In the following pages, an attempt shall be made, inspired by Paul Verhaeghe (1999), to shed light on it by looking into Freud's preoccupations in the days, and nights, of *Dreams'* conception—the time between 1895 and its publishing in 1900.

Action, identification, and phantasy: the road to the dream-book

In the discussion of *Studies*, it was seen how Freud defined the essence of hysteria as the displacement of energy, that is, the expression of psychic reality by a *false connection*. By the time of *Dreams*, however, the notion of such abreaction had disappeared almost completely, along with the idea of false connections. According to Paul Verhaeghe (1999, p. 15), in the years after *Studies* Freud became increasingly disillusioned with abreaction, as the cathartic release of affects just would not put an end to their supply, indicating a more fundamental, structural level of pathology, generating energy beyond the remembered trauma.

This turn towards what shall here be called "structure" can be found indicated at least as early as the 52nd letter to Wilhelm Fliess (December 6, 1896), interestingly also containing the seeds of what will become the metapsychological chapter 7 of *Dreams*. Here, Freud draws a distinction between *Abreagieren*, pointing towards energetic release and *Agieren*, implying rather structural reproduction:

> A hysterical attack is not a discharge but an *action*; and it retains the original characteristic of every action—of being a means to the reproduction of pleasure ... Attacks of giddiness and fits of weeping—all these are aimed at *another person*—but mostly at the prehistoric, unforgettable other person who is never equalled by any one later. (1950a, p. 239)

Fast forward a few years to his 125th letter (December 9, 1899) to Fliess, and one finds another such "structural" notion of hysteria as defined by *identification*:

> Hysteria (and its variant, obsessional neurosis) is allo-erotic: its main path is identification with the person loved. (1950a, p. 280)

As such, the hitherto established relation between energetic trauma and hysteria is destabilised, and one indeed sees Freud, from the aforementioned letter 52 at least until his letter 69, in which he famously admits to no longer believing in "my *neurotica*" (ibid., p. 259), profoundly preoccupied with the question of the nature of the traumatic aetiology of hysteria.

In this preoccupation, certain developments stand out, prominently one in "*draft K*" of January 1896 (ibid., p. 220). Here, a primary trauma is thought to establish, not so much an expressible image as a "gap in the psyche", covered over by a "boundary idea", a phantasy of sorts which "represents the repressed memory in the process of thought" and which, in the words of Paul Verhaeghe (1999, p. 40) "can afterwards become an appropriate target for repression as such".

Around the same time, in articles and letters immediately following *Studies*, such as "Heredity and the Aetiology of the Neuroses", Freud insistently stresses trauma as something to be established *retroactively*, reaching back in order to grasp something originally undefined:

> I believe I can see that *this inverse relation between the psychical effect of the memory and of the event contains the reason for the memory remaining unconscious.* (1896a, p. 154)

And similarly in letter 69, concerning the original trauma:

> It seems to have become once again arguable that it is only later experiences that give the impetus to phantasies, which then hark back to childhood. (1950a, p. 260)

The double nature of the Wunschregung

Acting, identification, phantasy—all are terms indicating something other than a mere accumulation of affect, pointing rather to a less time-bound, less material structure. It is interesting to note that from writing primarily of impulses, energy, and affects seeking discharge when depicting the nature of trauma, after these preoccupations and in the major works that follow (*Dreams*, but also *The Psychopathology of Everyday Life* (1901b) and *Jokes and Their Relation to the Unconscious* (1905c)), the until then rather underdeveloped notion of the *unconscious wish* (1895d, p. 302), as discussed earlier, and its means of expression silently come to take that place.

As such, the wish can be said to be the central concern of the works of this period, defining other central concepts such as the unconscious, defences, and the *I*, as did the notion of "strangulated affect" in the earlier works.

On the basis of this assumption, the nature of the wish as apparent in *Dreams* shall now be examined, in order to extract from it the contour of a new "structural" vision of the unconscious coexisting in the aforementioned bifurcation with the "dynamic" perspective of the earlier works, splitting the nature of the *I*.[1] In the former, the wish will look like a form seeking reproduction, overdetermining the *I* in it, whereas the latter implies an unconscious as impulse, dynamically defined by a now logically primary current *I* confronted with past versions of itself.

Locating the dream-wish

By now it should be clear how an unconscious wish is taken to be the driving force in the production of the dream, and we can now add— one that is furthermore said to be both immortal (1900a, p. 556) and infantile (p. 546). However, as many commentators have noted (e.g., Erikson, 1954, p. 15; Eysenck, 1985, p. 37; Welsh, 1994, p. 35), it is curious that most, if not all, of the dream-wishes excavated throughout *Dreams* should be, in the words of Erik Erikson, no more than preconscious. Time and again, Freud presents as motivation for dreams trifles over professional issues, grudges over minor slights, cravings for certain foods, etc.—so much so that Freud feels the need to stress how "the wishes which are represented in dreams as fulfilled are not always present-day wishes" (1900a, p. 249). This tendency in the definition of the wish seems to count each and any psychical striving, the unconsciousness of which is defined only relatively by its distance from conscious waking thinking, as is apparent from passages such as the following:

> Dreams frequently seem to have more than one meaning. Not only, as our examples have shown, may they include several wish-fulfilments one alongside the other; but a succession of meanings or wish-fulfilments may be superimposed on one another, the bottom one being the fulfilment of a wish dating from earliest childhood. (ibid., p. 219)

The infantile wish, then, is simply one like any other, but located, so to speak, at the farthest end of the psychic wish-container, the most present wish being the wish to sleep (ibid., p. 233). As such, certain authors have drawn the logical conclusion that the wishes satisfied by the dream must be simply located in the latent material (Marcus, 1999, p. 3) and have, as in *Studies*, possibly been at least preconscious at some point (Verhaeghe, 1999, p. 136). This notion of the unconscious continues the scheme of *Entwurf* in which the *I* and the repressed are now simply renamed *Pcs.* and *Ucs.* Furthermore, it harmonises with the regressive scheme of representations being translated back and forth, reachable by unwinding the fabric of the manifest dream into its constituent strings of associations. Such a reading finds its clear justification in certain central passages of the book:

> We have introduced a new class of psychical material between the manifest content of dreams and the conclusions of our enquiry: namely, their *latent* content, or (as we say) the "dream-thoughts", arrived at by means of our procedure. It is from these

dream-thoughts and not from a dream's manifest content that we disentangle its meaning. (1900a, p. 277)

However, the existence in other passages of a notion of the unconscious wish as something quite different from the repressed of *Studies* is difficult to deny. Here Freud points towards something never realised, resembling the unrepressed, structural unconscious hinted at in his correspondence with Fliess, revealing itself in passages such as the following:

> The memories on the basis of which the unconscious wish brings about the release of affect were never accessible to the *Pcs.*, and consequently the release of the affect attaching to those memories cannot be inhibited either. It is for the very reason of this generation of affect that these ideas are now inaccessible even by way of the preconscious thoughts on to which they have transferred their wishful force. (ibid., p. 604)

The unconscious: structure or impulse?

I would argue that the duality of perspective now fluctuating in the depiction of the unconscious dream-wish, placing it in the repressed or a beyond of the repressed, respectively implying a "dynamic" and "structural" perspective, lies already in the very word Freud often uses for it: *Wunschregung*. As such, the *Standard Edition*'s "wishful impulse" (e.g., ibid., p. 554), implicitly giving priority to the impulse-part of it, does not do justice to such duplicitous neologism, perhaps better read simply as "wish-impulse". We know from *Entwurf* the nature of "impulses" as energy striving for expression, that is, *abreaction*. How about the "wish"? A more elaborate definition by Freud is as "an experience of satisfaction":

> ... the mnemic image of which remains associated thenceforward with the memory trace of the excitation produced by the need. As a result of the link that has thus been established, next time this need arises a psychical impulse will at once emerge which will seek to re-cathect the mnemic image of the perception and to re-evoke the perception itself, that is to say, to re-establish the situation of the original satisfaction ... the reappearance of the perception is the fulfilment of the wish. (ibid., p. 565)

The *wish*, then, is from this perspective not for the satisfaction as such, the *abreaction* which the need-impulse seeks, but the very reproduction or repetition of a situation by imaginary identity—a medium, an *"action ... a means to reproducing pleasure"*. The actual impulse appears now to be the one running from the need to the "mnemic image", not the affects that may or may not arise in an *I* when thus situated (compare Freud, 1915c, p. 118).

In the "dynamic" perspective of *Studies*, the "content" of the unconscious apparatus appeared to be "impulses", that is *Affekten* (G. W., 2), experienced when coupled with representations as what one might call latent "intentions" of the subject striving for actualisation. Now the question arises as to what produces such impulses: another "impulse", the endogenously arising need, or the very structure of the situation sought re-established? Is the wish the medium of impulses, or do impulses arise from wishes? Such perspectival doubling of the wish-impulse compound as it exists in the psychic apparatus into what may tentatively be called impulse and wish furthermore raises the question as to whether the dream *in itself* qua structural reproduction constitutes the fulfilment of a wish, or merely presents a wish as fulfilled, that is an "impulse" as "satisfied"?

Stealing the wheelbarrow: the unconscious surface

This paradox finds tangible form in the repetition of dream-wishes resulting in *unpleasure*, since "impressions of earliest childhood ... strive to achieve reproduction, from their very nature and irrespectively perhaps of their actual content" (1900a, p. 245), the prime example of this being dreams depicting a *punishment* of the dreamer (ibid., p. 558). The form of such dreams implies both pleasure in the repressed and a need for punishment resulting in unpleasure in the *I*, with both being established reciprocally in the same *unconscious* wish. In order to explain such a phenomenon, Freud proposes a theoretical dissociation of the conceptual pair of conscious and unconscious from that of *I* and repressed (p. 558), the latter pair mirroring the representational centres of the anthropology of *Studies*.

The unconscious wish as defined within the new "structural" perspective, established between the systemic concepts of conscious and unconscious, now materialises in a dimension other than the one defined by compatibility or agreeableness, that is, by its nature of impulse as perceived by the *I*. Instead, it begins to appear better defined as a structure merely built from its raw materials, and their associated preconscious representations.

The very form or "surface" of the dream would now bear the aim of the unconscious wish as reproduction. And surely, in a footnote added to *Dreams* in 1925, Freud states, seemingly contradicting what was quoted earlier about the latent material as the dream's source:

> I used at one time to find it extraordinarily difficult to accustom readers to the distinction between the manifest content of dreams and the latent dream-thoughts. ... But now that analysts at least have become reconciled to replacing the manifest dream by the meaning revealed by its interpretation, many of them have become guilty of falling into another confusion which they cling to with equal obstinacy. They seek to find the essence of dreams in their latent content and in so doing they overlook the distinction between the latent dream-thoughts and the dream-work. (ibid., p. 506)

In this passage, the search for the place of the unconscious wish is pointed in the direction of the logic of the formation of the dream, rather than its material, towards the logic of the dreamwork and the voice of the conductor rather than the orchestra. On a Freudian note, this perspective seems excellently captured in a joke told by Slavoj Žižek:

> There is an old story about a worker suspected of stealing: every evening, as he leaves the factory, the wheelbarrow he rolls in front of him is carefully inspected. The guards can find nothing. It is always empty. Finally, the penny drops: what the worker is stealing are the wheelbarrows themselves ... (2008, p. 1)

The central question of concern, now, is not so much what lies beyond the form of the dream, but rather, echoing Freud's inaugural question: *what is the nature of the entity determining the form of transition? That is, from latent to manifest content?* What arises now is a perspective from which the wish *envelopes* the dream, structuring it and lending it its very form, but wholly contingent on the latent material as its building blocks, simultaneously their driving core and the essence of their very surface, hidden in plain sight, well likened to the continuous core-surface of the topological torus:

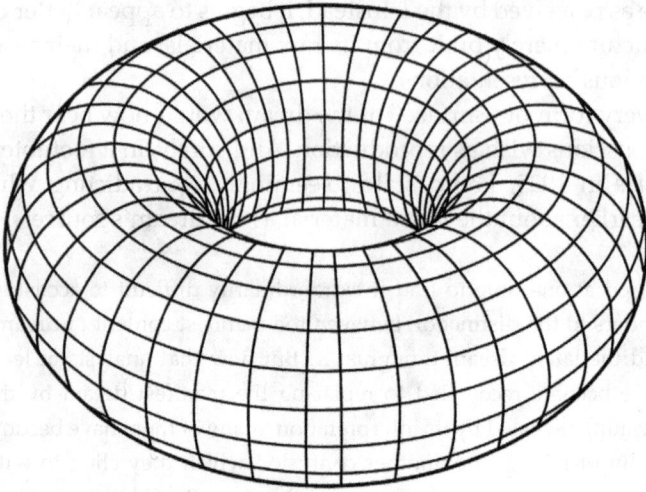

Figure 5.   Torus.

An I never dreamt of

On the basis of this discussion of the nature of the medium in which the *I* is enveloped in *Dreams*, we are now in a position to explicitly turn our attention towards the nature of the *I*. It is first of all interesting to note the practically complete lack of recourse to it as an explanatory entity in *Dreams* (Laplanche & Pontalis, 1973, p. 135). Freud does speak of the censorship, the wish to sleep, and the secondary revision as "achievements of the I", implying the somewhat personified *I* of *Studies*. However, such mechanisms are subsequently depicted in mechanistic terms without elaborating the consequences of such "belonging" to the *I*, rendering the idea of an "owner" of it redundant.

On the other hand, the *I* as the structurally defined *substantial* entity of associative definition established in *Entwurf* still makes up, I would argue, a point in the same dialectical core of the psychic apparatus as in earlier works. When Freud writes that "The wishes that are fulfilled" in the dream "are invariably the ego's wishes" (1900a, p. 267), this cannot but be read, in light of the earlier exposition, on two levels, both implying a continuity between *I* and unconscious: first, as in *Studies*, the unconscious as "repressed" is an impulse arisen in an earlier state of the *I*, now by definition incompatible (e.g., ibid., p. 248). Second, the wishes of the *I* are implicitly directed "around" those of the unconscious as "structure". How so?

As could be said of the symptom, the central formation of the unconscious in *Studies*, Freud now states that dreams are:

> ... completely egoistical. Whenever my own ego does not appear in the content of the dream, but only some extraneous person, I may safely assume that my own ego lies concealed, by identification, behind this other person; I can insert my ego into the context. On other occasions, when my own ego does appear in the dream, the situation in which it occurs may teach me that some other person lies concealed, by identification, behind my ego ... Thus my ego may be represented in a dream several times over, now directly and now through identification with extraneous persons. (ibid., p. 322)

This is perhaps explained by the itinerary of the wish having gone through *Pcs.* where the "content" of the *I* is located. On the other hand, the *I* appears again as the experiencing dreamer, meeting the manifest dream in *P.* through *Cs.*, decentring it from its own essence through a doubling detaching its "functional" definition as observer from its substance. By entering as an actor, a carrier of attributes, into all stations of the dreamwork, the aforementioned overdetermination by the structural *Ucs.*, as established on a level different from that of the dynamics of *I* and repressed, seems to reach to the very core of the *I* as a medium of wish-fulfilment. As put by Jean-Michel Rabaté (2007, p. 18), with the dream "What Freud offers us ... could be called the 'grammar of egoistic overdetermination,' in which the active and passive voices keep revolving around a mobile subjective center."

Following Mikkel Borch-Jacobsen (1988), the central question with respect to the *I* in Freud's earlier works was its *what*—its values, its fears and hopes—and its functions. Now, decentred from its own definition, another question arises, hinted at in the implicit preoccupation with social structures and misrecognition in *Studies*: that of its *who*.

Identifying the dreamer

Identification, it can now be argued, becomes perhaps *the* central notion with respect to the nature of the *I* in *Dreams*, as "not simply one psychical mechanism among others, but the operation itself whereby the human subject is constituted" (Laplanche & Pontalis, 1973, p. 206), the "*Grundbegriff* of psychoanalysis" (Borch-Jacobsen, 1988, p. 10). The question then arises: what status may be attributed to identification in

Dreams? Freud himself is ambiguous on this point, but I would argue that this can again be understood as a shifting between the two perspectives running through the work, this time manifesting itself in notions of identification as either *motivated* or *motivating*.

On the one hand, identification is seen merely as a tool of the censor, allowing the repressed impulse access to expression, as in the case of the dream of the sick Otto:

> I must have been prepared at all times in my *Ucs.* to identify myself with Professor R., since by means of that identification one of the immortal wishes of childhood—the megalomaniac wish—was fulfilled. (Freud, 1900a, p. 556)

In the same vein, Freud more categorically states that:

> [I]dentification is not simple imitation but *assimilation* on the basis of a similar aetiological pretension; it expresses a resemblance and is derived from a common element which remains in the unconscious. (ibid., p. 150)

We see here the dynamics of the approaches of *the repressed*—an "impulse" as the "common element", finding its way to expression by means of displacement through identification.

At other times, however, identification appears aetiologically primary with respect to the substance of the *I*, and thus to the generation of impulses as established on the "dynamic" continuum. This is seen, for instance, in Freud's dream of his uncle Joseph, in which, on the basis of a childhood prophecy that he would himself become a minister:

> In mishandling my two learned and eminent colleagues because they were Jews, and in treating the one as a simpleton and the other as a criminal, I was behaving as though I were the Minister, I had put myself in the Minister's place. (ibid., p. 193)

The same tendency is seen elaborated in the dream of the butcher's wife:

> "I wanted to give a supper-party, but I had nothing in the house but a little smoked salmon. I thought I would go out and buy something, but remembered then that it was Sunday afternoon and all the shops would be

shut. Next I tried to ring up some caterers, but the telephone was out of
order. So I had to abandon my wish to give a supper-party." (ibid., p. 147)

Freud initially identifies two wishes in this dream, both representing
"the strictly reactive 'desire' of the ego" (Borch-Jacobsen, 1988, p. 11).
First, the dreamer admits to a wish to prove Freud's thesis of the dream
being a wish-fulfilment wrong, and thus depicts her wish to have a
supper-party as frustrated. Upon elaboration, however, it turns out that
the supper-party was a request from a friend the butcher had taken some
liking to, whose favourite dish, although she denies herself eating it too
often, is *smoked salmon*. This now renders the message of the dream:

> A likely thing! I'm to ask you to come and eat in my house so that
> you may get stout and attract my husband still more! I'd rather
> never give another supper-party. (Freud, 1900a, p. 148)

Freud, however, is not quite satisfied yet. These are wishes of the
dreamer, but what about the wishes of *the dream itself*? He returns to
his inaugural question, pointing towards an unconscious nature of the
I: what lies *in between*—why would a wish to frustrate the friend depict
the dreamer's *own* frustration?

The quest for an answer is spurred on by the discovery that the dreamer
"at the same time as she was occupied with her dream of the renunciation
of a wish, was also trying to bring about a renounced wish (for the caviar
sandwich) in real life" (ibid., p. 149). As such, Freud concludes, "She had
put herself in her friend's place ... she had 'identified' herself with her
friend" (p. 149). Why? Due to her place in the eyes of the butcher:

> Identification is most frequently used in hysteria to express a com-
> mon *sexual* element. A hysterical woman identifies herself in her
> symptoms most readily—though not exclusively—with people
> with whom she has had sexual relations or with people who have
> had sexual relations with the same people as herself. (ibid., p. 150)

Between the symptom and dream denying herself satisfaction and her
latent rivalrous wishes, Freud pins the *relation* between the dream-*I*
and the image of the other, the rival, in the strictly unconscious structure present in the very form of the dream. We have here a *problematique*
(Laplanche, 1999b) of the sexual, femininity bounded by a fantasmatic

structure defining a desire (Verhaeghe, 1999), an unconscious *question* rather than a primal conflict (Deleuze, 1994, p. 143): "*What is wanted of me?*"—and its imagined answer by the beloved butcher. By depicting an *I* with a frustrated wish, not only does the dreamer act on her jealousy towards her rival, she also takes her place, exposing the identificational striving underpinning that very rivalrous feeling.

As such, the *what* of the dreamer is not absolute, but established in this case in an unconscious triangular structure defining its *who*, centred on the denied wish as an Archimedean point of resemblance, a "common element" ordering dynamic relations between the three actors in this play of love and jealousy.

Trimethylamine: the case of Sigmund Freud

To further strengthen the notion of the unconscious wish as a matter of structure defining the "who" of the *I*, in the following I shall argue as to its relevance even for Freud's "dream of dreams", his specimen dream which he imagined would win him the aforementioned plaque: that of Irma's injection:

> *A large hall—numerous guests, whom we were receiving.—Among them was Irma. I at once took her on one side, as though to answer her letter and to reproach her for not having accepted my "solution" yet. I said to her: "If you still get pains, it's really only your fault." She replied: "If you only knew what pains I've got now in my throat and stomach and abdomen—it's choking me" —I was alarmed and looked at her. She looked pale and puffy. I thought to myself that after all I must be missing some organic trouble. I took her to the window and looked down her throat, and she showed signs of recalcitrance, like women with artificial dentures. I thought to myself that there was really no need for her to do that.—She then opened her mouth properly and on the right I found a big white patch; at another place I saw extensive whitish grey scabs upon some remarkable curly structures which were evidently modelled on the turbinal bones of the nose.—I at once called in Dr. M., and he repeated the examination and confirmed it. ... Dr. M. looked quite different from usual; he was very pale, he walked with a limp and his chin was clean-shaven. ... My friend Otto was now standing beside her as well, and my friend Leopold was percussing her through her bodice and saying: "She has a dull area low down on the left." He also indicated that a portion of the skin on the left shoulder*

was infiltrated. (I noticed this, just as he did, in spite of her dress.) ... M.
said: "There's no doubt it's an infection, but no matter; dysentery will
supervene and the toxin will be eliminated." ... We were directly aware,
too, of the origin of the infection. Not long before, when she was feeling
unwell, my friend Otto had given her an injection of a preparation of pro-
pyl, propyls ... propionic acid ... trimethylamin (and I saw before me the
formula for this printed in heavy type) ... Injections of that sort ought not
to be made so thoughtlessly. ... And probably the syringe had not been
clean. (Freud, 1900a, p. 107)

Freud's subsequent analysis of this dream seems to follow the same tra-
jectory as that of the butcher's wife's dream. First, in formally express-
ing "concern about my own and other people's health—professional
conscientiousness" (ibid., p. 120) the dream proves an allusion to the
contrary from the preceding day wrong. Second, following associations outwards through an intricate web of persons, Freud elaborates
on how the dream expresses revenge at certain rivals annoying him,
and an exemption from responsibility in the eyes of his superiors for the
outcome of Irma's treatment (ibid., p. 118).

These can now be said to be *dynamic* wishes of "the dreamer", in line
with the two first interpretations of the dream of the butcher's wife,
centred solidly upon the *I* Freud knows himself to be. However, he
stops short here, stating simply how "I myself know the points from
which further trains of thought could be followed. But considerations
which arise in the case of every dream of my own restrain me from pur-
suing my interpretative work" (ibid., p. 121). One is moved to wonder:

> [H]ow is it that Freud, who later on will develop the function of
> unconscious desire, is here content, for the first step in his dem-
> onstration, to present a dream which is entirely explained by the
> satisfaction of a desire which one cannot but call preconscious, and
> even entirely conscious? (Lacan, 1988, p. 151)

Similarly, on the very opposite end of the theoretical scale, Erik Erikson
agrees that "[T]he wish demonstrated here is not more than preconscious," but that the dream implies a "theme of sexuality" not "carried
through beyond a point which is clearly intended to be understood by
the trained reader and to remain vague to the untrained one" (1954,
p. 15). And further, in the pointed words of Hans Eysenck: "The wish

involved in the dream is a perfectly conscious and present one, and this goes completely contrary to Freud's hypothesis" (1985, p. 37).

In order to locate the point from which the structurally unconscious wish can be reached, prominent commentators (Anzieu, 1987; Copjec, 1994; Felman, 1993; Lacan, 1988; Weber, 1982, etc.) have pointed to Freud's own notion of the "navel of the dream":

> There is often a passage in even the most thoroughly interpreted dream which has to be left obscure; this is because we become aware during the work of interpretation that at that point there is a tangle of dream-thoughts which cannot be unravelled and which moreover adds nothing to our knowledge of the content of the dream. This is the dream's navel, the spot where it reaches down into the unknown. ... It is at some point where this meshwork is particularly close that the dream-wish grows up, like a mushroom out of its mycelium. (1900a, p. 525)

As pointed out by Melvyn Hill, a navel implies a womb, and thus "that the unconscious 'meshwork' of thinking is the womb of the dream it gives birth to" (1980, p. 208)—and, one might add, that of the *I*. The navel is not of the order of the "content of the dream", neither is it itself "the unknown" beyond. It is a point of transition, allowing the latter to condense into manifest form, an empty point of structuration allowing a reciprocal flow of life between one world and another. What better way to define the unconscious as the structuring medium of the form of the dream?

Furthermore, Freud notes how

> In most dreams it is possible to detect a central point which is marked by peculiar sensory intensity ... This central point is as a rule the direct representation of the wish-fulfilment. (1900a, p. 561)

If one opts, as we shall do here, for such reading of the navel of the dream as an unsignifying materialisation of the structural wish bounding the original unconscious, supposed to appear with peculiar sensory intensity, it is immediately identifiable in the case of Irma's injection. At a most remarkable point here, Freud sees appearing before him, "printed in heavy type" the formula for *trimethylamine*:

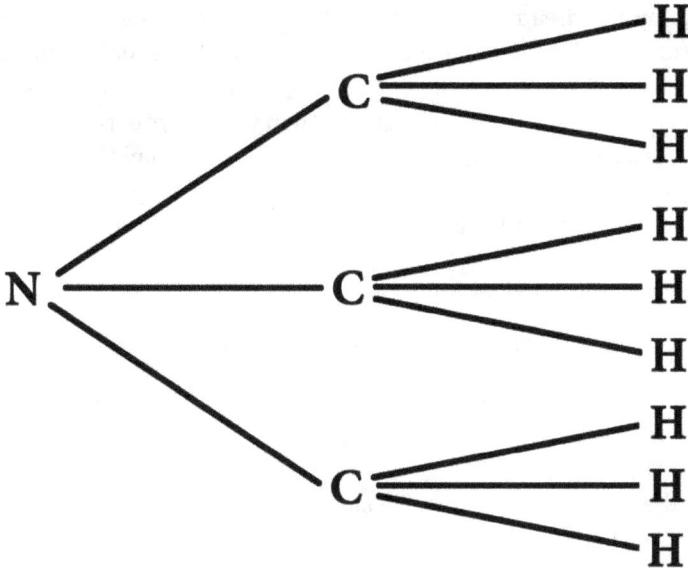

Figure 6.   Chemical formula for trimethylamine as it, according to D. Anzieu (1987) and J. Lacan (1988), appeared to Freud in the dream of Irma's injection.

This formula, with Freud's *I* as the central N, maps the recurrent spread of relational triads, that the reader will have seen unfold in Freud's meticulous associations to his dreams, insisting in its visual prominence, that

> These threes which we keep encountering, again and again, that's where, in the dream, the unconscious is—what is outside all of the subjects. (Lacan, 1988, p. 159)

From this formula a myriad of suggestions as to what characters from Freud's past are to be placed in which positions have sprung (See Bronfen, 1998 for a review), all of them agreeing that the characters in the dream "are significant, in that each of them is the site of an identification whereby the ego is formed" (Lacan, 1988, p. 156). As such, the unconscious wish is not so much a matter of repressed aspects of the *I*, as it is, in the words of Lacan, suggestive of the *Verdichtung* of light producing the dream, "a spectral decomposition of the function of the ego" (ibid., p. 165). Furthermore, in line with the sexual nature of the unconscious in the dream of the butcher's wife, Freud associates the tri-methylamine to *sexuality itself*, as central in the "chemistry of the sexual processes" (1900a, p. 116). As noted by Jeffrey Mehlman (1976), the very structure of the dream thus mirrors the sexual forcing its way into the innocent world of the neurotic, retrospectively revealing its omnipresence in the unknowing *I*.

Conclusion: the egoistical unconscious

In summary, it seems that a double perspective runs from the nature of the unconscious wish throughout *Dreams*, splitting the nature of the *I* along the way.

On the one hand, we see a *"dynamic"* unconsciousness defined from the perspective of an *I* struggling to censor the repressed, its depiction following the scheme of *Studies*: potentially representable, impulse-like in nature, defined as disagreeable by its incompatibility with the *I* and thus repressed. As such, though unconscious in a dynamic sense, in the scheme of *Dreams* it appears to lie in *Pcs.*, however inaccessible, from where it seeks discharge in the form of abreaction, implying, as in *Studies*, an agentive *I* as its counterpart.

This "dynamic" perspective of Freud's earlier works arguably implies a reified, structurally primary *I* defining the nature of unconsciousness and its wishes. Such a vision of the *I* now appears in *Dreams* to coexist with a notion of identification in the unconscious as the mainspring of wish fulfilment. The latter in turn desubstantiates the primary *I*, by implying a *structural* overdetermination of both the *I* and the repressed in an unhindered mode of operation of the system *Ucs.* (Gammelgaard, 2016). Here the distinction between *I* and repressed, defining dynamic, "motivational" unconsciousness, gives way to a structural *Ucs./Pcs.*-dichotomy and an unconscious constitutionally unfit for concrete representation, though implicitly present in the very structure of the dream. The content here, in the words of Gilles Deleuze (1994, p. 124), is not merely a past present, but a "pure past", an unrepressed unconscious (Fayek, 2014) immanent in the present as a virtual essence. As such it is unrepresentable, *bewußtseinsunfähig*, and "insists" (Lacan, 1957) in repetition by shaping the dream in its own image. As put by Jeffrey Mehlman (1976, p. 42), this is not so much "a latent content *beneath* the manifest [as] a latent organisation *of* the manifest", in which it is "the masked, the disguised or the costumed which turns out to be the truth of the uncovered" (Deleuze, 1994, p. 29)—the *dreamwork* connecting latent and manifest content. Whereas the wishes, that is the representational organisations of the flows of desire in the psychic apparatus, in *Studies* and *Entwurf* were objective stationary elements, such objects are now also relativised, assembled within an unconscious desire enveloping them. In *Dreams*, one sees the *I* defined, on a structural level, not so much by *having* or *not having* a wish, as by *being*, that is *embodying* a wish of another level of organisation.

In light of this duality of perspective, it appears even clearer how the dynamic perspective of *Studies* and *Entwurf* to a large extent took its departure in the reasoning of the *I* itself, allowing it the centring stability of an Archimedean point from where unconsciousness becomes a matter of incompatibility with the thus logically primary *I* guarding desires that are essentially its own. Indeed, one may concur with Anna Freud—though surely not in the way she intended—in viewing *Dreams* as an "id psychology", because the structural perspective of the newly defined *system Ucs.* is simultaneously present as an overdetermining explanatory entity.

Note

1. Note that this distinction is one I draw, not simply reflecting that between what has in psychoanalytic literature been called the "dynamic" and "system" unconscious.

CHAPTER THREE

On Narcissism: history of the monad

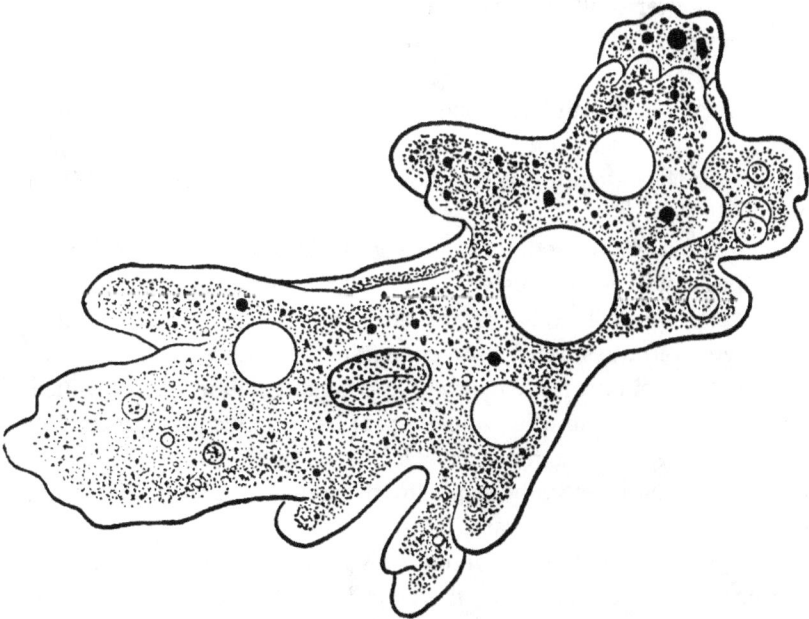

Figure 7. The I as libidinal amoeba, relating to objects as by pseudo-podia (1914c, p. 75).

Preface

In keeping with the structure set out in the general introduction, this chapter shall cover Freud's writings from 1900 until 1920. Anything more than the most cursory reading of these works, however, is sure to reveal the almost chaotic nature of the metapsychological developments of the period, not easily reducible to the long span of time in which they unfold, or to the internal controversies in the psychoanalytic movement during these years. New concepts appear with little introduction while others are left behind without mention, and familiar concepts change their meanings unnoticed, intermingled with seemingly contradictory notions—often within the same texts (see Baranger, 1991).

Confronted with material of this kind, two readings seem equally justified. On the one hand, one may read for consistency, an "ego reading", stitching together a narrative capable of integrating disparate tendencies, with the danger of taking such scaffolding for the building itself. On the other, one may undertake a "psychoanalytic reading", specifically attentive to inconsistency, taking breaks in meaning and changes in perspective to be an integral part of the content expressed.

This chapter shall take the second route capable of revealing, seemingly beyond Freud's intention, how the paradoxical duplicity of perspective that characterised the Freudian *I* in the two previous chapters repeats itself in the midst of incoherence. Here, beyond formal and historical challenges to consolidation during these years, the very object of Freud's theory appears once again itself to resist unambiguous encapsulation.

Unfortunately, depicting every new aspect of Freud's *I* in this period is beyond the reach of this volume. Instead, its nature shall be sought in the *I*'s relation to what is arguably the central, "driving" concept of the years in question: *the drive* ("instinct" in the *S. E.*, "*Trieb*" in the *G. W.*). The notion of a drive may appear to exclude the relevance of an *I*. However, as paradigmatically proposed by Jacques Lacan (1958), quite the opposite is the case. Unlike instincts proper (*G. W.*, 10, p. 294), drives essentially imply mediation in expression and influence in development, situated as such exactly in interaction with an *I*. Indeed, individual development now becomes a key term, as Freud, during the period instated by the *Three Essays on the Theory of Sexuality* (henceforth *Essays*) of 1905 and culminating in the reconfiguration of the theory of the drives in 1920's *Beyond the Pleasure Principle*, seeks to integrate the drive in an ontogenetic scheme. It therefore seems natural to perceive the writings from 1905 until 1920 as a whole, and it is on these years that this chapter shall focus.

James Strachey (Freud, 1915c, p. 114) emphasises how the sexual drive (*G. W.*, *5*, p. 38: *Sexualtrieb*), the *libido*, is not freely mentioned until the *Essays*, from where however it soon replaces earlier notions of endogenous stimuli and wishful impulses. Yet the continuity with these is clearly seen in passages such as the following from "The Unconscious":

> The nucleus of the *Ucs.* consists of instinctual representatives which seek to discharge their cathexis; that is to say, it consists of wishful impulses. (Freud, 1915e, p. 186)

Consequently, the content of intrapsychic conflictual material is redefined, requiring a corresponding reconceptualisation of the *I* as a structuring entity in ontogenesis. This is initially done by defining the *I* through the *ego-instincts* (*G. W.*, *8*, p. 97: *den Ichtrieben*), representing the adaptive needs of the organism.

Several authors (e.g., Cohen, 2007; Green, 2001; Markotic, 2001), however, point out how a radically different developmental scheme emerges with the introduction of the notion of an *ego-libido* (*G. W.*, *10*, p. 141: *Ichlibido*), collapsing the two sides of the previous dynamics— the ego and the libido—into one. The introduction of an ego-libido is a consequence of certain aspects of Freud's notion of *narcissism*, in which the *I* takes itself as love-object, rendering this, in the words of Willy Baranger, "one of the most problematic and obscure in all psychoanalytic theory" (1991, p. 109). As pointed out by André Green (2001, p. 49), most psychoanalytic schools have handled the paradox of the subject becoming its own object by introducing auxiliary concepts such as a "self" or "identity" (Yorke, 1991), effectively banishing narcissism proper to a primitive developmental *stage* before object relations (Moncayo, 2008, p. 4). However, as Baranger further notes, "[T]hough Freud defines narcissism principally as a specific vicissitude of libido, it cannot be isolated from a concomitant vicissitude of objects and psychic agencies or structures" (1991, p. 121). Extracts like the latter point towards a more psychologically complex perspective on narcissism as rather a *structure* in development, implying always already highly specific relations to objects, not easily consolidated with any linear ontogenetic narrative. In keeping with the aforementioned strategy of "psychoanalytic reading", the complexity of narcissism shall therefore be elaborated at some length in this chapter insofar as it defines the nature of the *I*.

As such, the reader shall once more find him- or herself confronted with two different, however interwoven, stories of the *I*: on the one hand, a story of progressive psychic differentiation of opposed drives, on the other one of their essential unity. On the one hand, a history of the *I* as subject of reality, on the other one of it as object of desire. The ensuing depiction of such developmental schemes shall to a large extent be structured by a distinction drawn by Jean Laplanche (1987) between two visions of the *I* in Freud's work, as these seem well fitted to capture the nature of the *I* within each scheme: one establishes the *I* *metonymically* as intrapsychic agent of the interest of the organism, implying a substantial similarity or continuity between the two "instances". The other involves a merely *metaphorical* derivation of the *I* as image or reflection of the organism, implying a qualitative difference between the two.

The theory of the drives

Due to the importance of the notion of the drive for the works of the period discussed in this chapter, a quick survey of the nature of the drive, primarily as depicted in *Essays* (1905d), is initially called for.

The nature and components of the drives

Freud consistently depicts the drive as an essentially sexual force or *energy* (ibid., p. 217). Given the name of *libido* (p. 135), it can be understood as a form of human desire best likened to *love*, making up one part of "all the organic instincts that operate in our mind", the remainder of which is differentially likened to *hunger* (1910i, p. 214). Phenomenologically, one may grasp such distinction by reflecting on the way in which physical pain may be unpleasant, but still be "pleasurable" if libidinally desired (1915c, p. 128).

Another paradigmatic example of the drive is the sexual pleasure in thumb sucking: "It was the child's first and most vital activity, his sucking at his mother's breast ... that must have familiarised him with this pleasure ... The need for repeating the sexual satisfaction now becomes detached from the need for taking nourishment" (1905d, p. 181).

Whereas the need is directed at the nourishment, the sexual drive is said to be *auto-erotic*, directed at the child's own body: the now "eroto-genic" lip zone (p. 180).

The drives thus arise as merely "leaning on" vital functions. Some-what confusingly, however, Freud also speaks of such *Lebenserhaltung dienenden Funktionen* (functions serving the preservation of life) as non-sexual "drives" with their "source in motor impulses" (ibid., p. 168, n. 1). Later these are to be named "ego-instincts" (Freud, 1910i, p. 214), but given the derived and perverting nature of the drive proper, the former are surely best understood simply as the adaptive bodily needs, the actual instincts, qua tied to "nutritive processes" (1905d, p. 217).

In line with such virtual derivation of the sexual source from the purely somatic, Freud in 1915 adds that "Although instincts are wholly determined by their origin in a somatic source, in mental life we know them only by their aims" (1915c, p. 123). Freud's definition of the aim, however, is ambiguous. One prevalent definition is that of its being "in every instance satisfaction, which can only be obtained by removing the state of stimulation at the source of the instinct" (ibid., p. 122)—that is, the ultimate removal of the sexual stimulation.

However, a somewhat different story appears in Freud's depiction of the formal displacements of the drive, such as from masochism to sad-ism (1905d, p. 157), pointing towards what may heuristically be called the "form" of the drive as something implying an aim in itself. Look-ing back at the example of thumb sucking, Freud notes that satisfaction establishes not simply a tendency to specific repetition of a need, but con-versely "a need of a repetition of the satisfaction ... We can therefore for-mulate a sexual aim in another way: it consists in replacing the projected sensation of stimulation in the erotogenic zone by an external stimulus which removes that sensation by producing a feeling of satisfaction" (ibid., p. 184). Here, the erotogenic zone acts rather as a scene for satisfac-tion, staging the drive as *act*, that is, a certain *form* of satisfaction merely projected onto it. The aim of the drive can thus be said to be both the final satisfaction, tied to the *source*, and a specific "scene" tied to its *object*, the thing in relation to which it achieves satisfaction (Laplanche, 1987, p. 22).

As the reader will notice, these two readings of the drive mirror the two readings of the *Wunschregung* in *Dreams*, as wish and impulse respectively, and shall again be seen to accompany two perspectives throughout the works of this period, implying two different perspec-tives on the *I*.

The maturation of the drives in the metonymic scheme

> The final outcome of sexual development lies in what is known as
> the normal sexual life of the adult, in which the pursuit of pleasure
> comes under the sway of the reproductive function and in which
> the component instincts, under the primacy of a single erotogenic
> zone, form a firm organization directed towards a sexual aim
> attached to some extraneous sexual object. (Freud in *Essays*, 1905d,
> p. 197, added 1915)

In light of the above quote, the central question concerning ontogenesis
now becomes: how does the drive, the energy of specifically human
attachment, whose object and organ originally coincide (1915c, p. 132),
become attached to the external world, that is, how does it become
object-oriented? As it turns out, this question implies taking a stand on
the place of the drive in the psychic apparatus, with consequences for
the nature of the *I*.

A fundamental developmental narrative in Freud's works in this
period is found already in *Essays*. Here Freud describes sexuality as
having two prominent phases, one can't have two primary phases an
infantile and a more mature one, the former introverted and the latter
extroverted so to speak, mediated by a phase of repression: "The sexual
instinct has hitherto been predominantly auto-erotic; it now finds a sexual object" (1905d, p. 207). In finding an object, the drive is qualitatively
changed, becoming now "so to say, altruistic" (p. 207). The change is
thought to occur around the fifth year of life (1908b, p. 171) with the
beginning of a "period of latency" in which aspects of infantile sexual
life are repressed and subsequently reshaped into a more socially acceptable form. Here sexual energy is deferred from its sexual use, since:

> ... these impulses would seem in themselves to be perverse—that
> is, to arise from erotogenic zones and to derive their activity from
> instincts which, in view of the direction of the subject's develop-
> ment, can only arouse unpleasurable feelings. They consequently
> evoke opposing mental forces (reacting impulses) which, in order
> to suppress this unpleasure effectively, build up the mental dams
> ... disgust, shame and morality. (1905d, p. 178)

Instead, the drives are now turned into an "affectionate current",
attached to adaptively necessary relations in the form, for instance, of
"affection, admiration and respect" (ibid., p. 200).

It is not, however, until 1910 that Freud explicitly identifies the *I* with such adaptive needs by naming these *ego-instincts*, furthermore defined as "those other instincts, which have as their aim the self-preservation of the individual" (1910i, p. 213). As such, the *I* is established as antithetical to, and a seat of resistance against, infantile sexuality. One hears here an echo of the developmental scheme of *Entwurf*, and indeed a very similar one is presented in "Formulations on the Two Principles of Mental Functioning" (1911b) (henceforth *Two Principles*) with the function of the *I*, in light of the new dualism, now displaced to the drive energising it, as illustrated below (page numbers in brackets referring to this work):

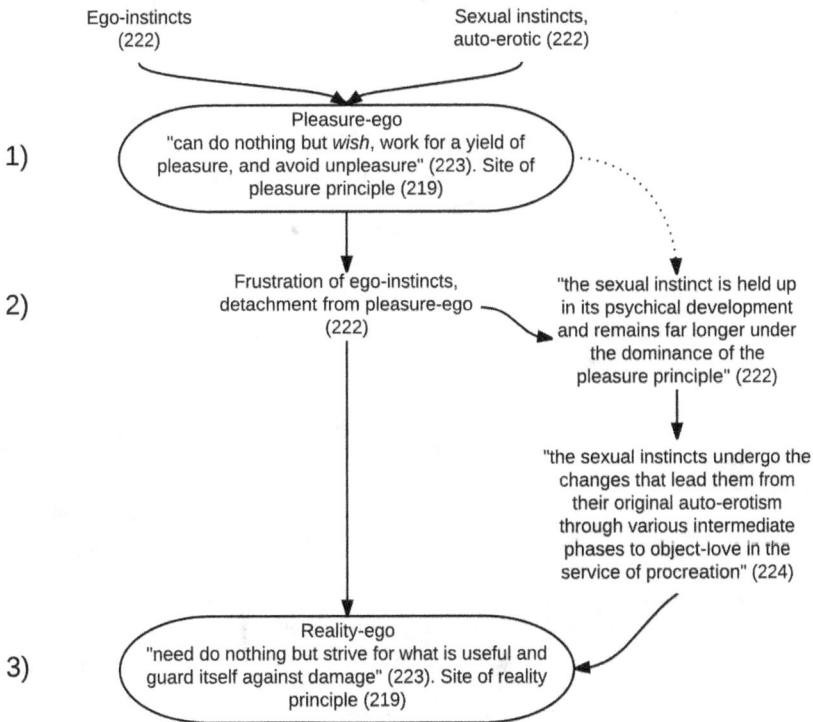

Figure 8.   1911: Formulations on the Two Principles of Mental Functioning.

At the basis of development the reader now finds the dualism of ego-instincts and sexual instincts. In the beginning (1), both reside in a *pleasure-ego*, an organising instance as in *Entwurf*, but fully under the sway of the pleasure principle. The transition to a *reality-ego* (3) organised around "a conception of the real circumstances in the external world" and the subsequent representations hereof (p. 219) is established as the ego-instincts are frustrated (2) by the pleasure-ego's "attempt at satisfaction by means of hallucination" (p. 219). The sexual instinct is now in opposition to the *I* as the seat of reality, and the struggle depicted in the *Essays* can commence. Another example of the same logic is found in "Instincts and Their Vicissitudes" (1915c) (henceforth *Vicissitudes*), as illustrated below (page numbers in brackets referring to this work):

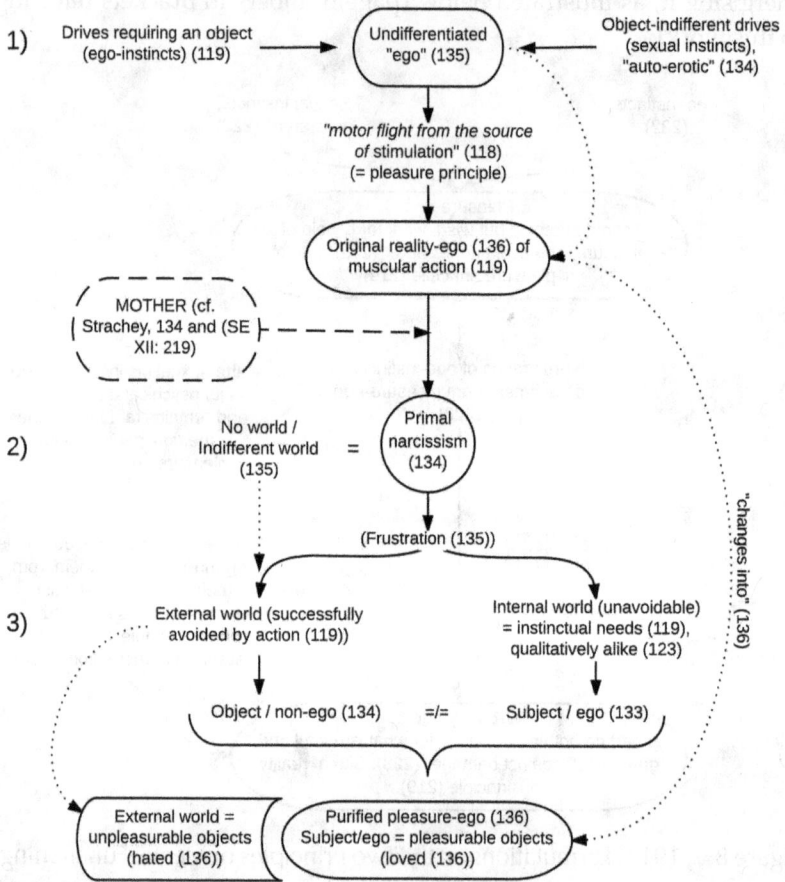

Figure 9.   1915: Instincts and Their Vicissitudes.

This time, development is only traced until the ("purified") pleasure-ego, and must be thought of as supplemented by subsequent steps in other texts (Laplanche & Pontalis, 1973, p. 320). Still, this is easily read as a narrative positing the drive in opposition to adaptation, while developing in conflict with adaptive tendencies in the organism, here real reflexive action and a distinction between subject and object. What is essential to this reading is the way in which the drive is here established in a conflictual relation between endogenously generated needs and the objective reality of the external world. At the outset (1), the sexual drives are now said to be "attached to the instincts of self-preservation, from which they only gradually become separated" (Freud, 1915c, p. 126). Such separation, however, is thought to be postponed by the fact that the reflexive motor actions of the child are complemented by the care of the mother. This results in a stage of "primal narcissism" (2) in which the child appears to himself perfectly self-sufficient, and in which—or exactly because—an outer world does not yet subjectively exist. Soon, however, the ego-instincts are bound to be frustrated by imperfections in maternal care, forcing a distinction between an inner and an outer world, respectively defined as modifiable by hallucination and motor action (3). Such distinction further entails a subjective distinction between ego and non-ego, but since the reality-principle has not yet been properly introduced, a reorganisation of the experiences of the *I* in accordance with the pleasure principle is instead undertaken (4): "In so far as the objects which are presented to it are sources of pleasure, it takes them into itself, 'introjects' them ... and, on the other hand, it expels whatever within itself becomes a cause of unpleasure" (p. 136).

The immediately apparent developmental scheme in both models above implies a *metonymical* displacement or derivation of separate fields or orders—heredity and influence, organism and society—to their homologous representatives *in* the psychic apparatus. The dualism is naturalised by attributing to each a separate form of energy—libido and ego-instinct. While the drive is depicted as an impulse with the body as its object, oblivious of reality, the complementary function of the outwardly oriented *I* becomes that of an agent of reality in the psychic space, essentially directing the drive towards adaptive outer aims.

The place of the drive in the psychic apparatus

> [T]wo views, seemingly equally well-founded, may be taken of
> the relation between the ego and sexuality. On the one view, the
> individual is the principal thing, sexuality is one of its activities
> and sexual satisfaction one of its needs; while on the other view the
> individual is a temporary and transient appendage to the quasi-
> immortal germ-plasm, which is entrusted to him by the process of
> generation. (Freud in *Vicissitudes*, 1915c, p. 125)

One now better understands James Strachey's choice of "instinct" as
a translation of Freud's *Trieb*. It seems obvious to read Freud's psychic
apparatus as a mere scene for an inner battle of adaptation, of perversion
and altruism, of a primitive pleasure-oriented *I* and its mature reality-
oriented opposite. The very notion of the drive as originally auto-erotic
implies a developmental narrative from introversion to extroversion,
from the perverse to the genital, the sterile to the reproductive, from the
"*beloved ego*" of the dream to the mature one of the dreamer.

Moving just a bit closer to the text, however, one begins to notice
how this harmoniously disharmonic developmental scheme on the surface of the theory is disturbed by passages complicating the place of the
drive in the psychic apparatus, and thus of the metonymic scheme in
general. In *Vicissitudes*, Freud firmly establishes the drive as:

> … a concept on the frontier between the mental and the somatic, as
> the psychical representative of the stimuli originating from within
> the organism and reaching the mind, as a measure of the demand
> made upon the mind for work in consequence of its connection
> with the body. (1915c, p. 121)[1]

That the drive is as such not itself the impulse of the organism, but its
psychical representative, appears easily graspable. This would seem to
establish the instinct-drive as essentially biological, attached to a stand-
in of sorts in the psychic apparatus—the drive proper. It seems harder,
however, to grasp how it is equally *on the frontier of the mental*, the ter-
minal field of the impulse, and thus just as irreducible to this, while
still being positively defined as a *psychical* representative. The exact
wording used by Freud on this point is not incidental, as it is repeated
verbatim elsewhere (e.g., 1911c, p. 74; & 1905d, p. 168). This problem

appears to be what is crystalised the same year in *The Unconscious* when Freud states how:

> An instinct can never become an object of consciousness—only the idea that represents the instinct can. Even in the unconscious, moreover, an instinct cannot be represented otherwise than by an idea. (1915e, p. 177)

When a drive is said to be unconscious, what is thus meant is "an instinctual impulse the ideational representative of which is unconscious" (1915c, p. 112). In *Repression*, also of 1915, Freud further writes of "representatives", which drives become "attached to", and of ideas "cathected" by drive-energy (1915d, p. 148). As such, the drive is not merely to be understood as the psychic representative, or metonymically derived "advocate" of the organic.

There now appear to be at least two probable readings of such a paradox, two solutions. On the one hand, one may read the drive *per se* as the organic source itself, its representative being its form or object as apparent in the psychic apparatus, stretching the drive out between these two realms. This would conform to the "dynamic" perspective as depicted in *Dreams*.

Alternatively, one may read Freud literally and see the drive as something like a form outside the mental, merely residing in its contents, formally driving their functions and charging them with libidinal energy. This would conform very well with the "structural" perspective in *Dreams*, rendering the drive exactly *the nucleus of the Ucs.* (1915e, p. 186), read as the "system *Ucs.*". This distinction between *Vorstellungen* (ideas) and drives understood as *structures* would make sense of passages such as in the aforementioned *Repression* where Freud defines "an instinctual representative" as an "idea or group of ideas which is cathected with a definite quota of psychical energy (libido or interest) coming from an instinct" (1915d, p. 152). And indeed, certain authors insist on the drive being a development of the notion of the wish in *Dreams* (Køppe & Olsen, 1983, p. 32).

Thus, on the one hand the drive is an essentially maladapted impulse, defined by its organic source, requiring restriction to facilitate maturation—a *Regung*. On the other, the drive is something beyond both the instinctual and the adaptive, which first and foremost shapes desire, and merely allows the passage of organic energy into the mental realm—a *Wunsch*. Such two perspectives seem to conform to the two sides of the aim of the drive as discussed earlier—discharge and scenery, pleasure and repetition.

In the same vein, other authors note that even though the vital sphere of the organism is part of Freud's theoretical developments of this period, one is struck by its general absence in the case histories and clinical vignettes. The adaptive function is here depicted more as a "stake or terrain of the defensive conflict rather than one of its dynamic components" (Laplanche & Pontalis, 1973, p. 147). By extension, others stress how it is the sexual sphere that is the sole concern of psychoanalysis, concern with the vital sphere being largely speculative (Køppe & Olsen, 1981, p. 352). And surely, Freud himself has his trouble upholding this drive-dualism. An amusing example is found in *On Narcissism: An Introduction* (1914c) (henceforth *Narcissism*) where Freud, in his attempts at arguing against Jung's energetic monism, blunders into a genuine case of kettle logic (emphasis added):[2]

1. "[A]n antithesis between ego-instincts and sexual instincts (a hypothesis to which we were *forcibly led by analysis of the transference neuroses*)" (p. 79).
2. "I should like at this point expressly to admit that the hypothesis of separate ego-instincts and sexual instincts (that is to say, the libido theory) *rests scarcely at all upon a psychological basis, but derives its principal support from biology*" (p. 79).
3. "They are not the bottom but the top of the whole structure, and they *can be replaced and discarded without damaging it*" (p. 77).

In several other passages (e.g., 1914c, p. 92; & 1915c, p. 123) Freud admits both that their separation is a hypothesis phenomenologically based on manifest psychic conflict, and that their primal unity must be conceived of as a myth (1905d, p. 219). Having displaced the function of adaptive subjectivity to the ego-instincts energising the *I* at certain times, this appears to confound the entire metonymic scheme, and with it the *I* of adaptation antagonistic to sexuality.

Whichever perspective one chooses, it now has consequences for how the relation between the *I* and the drive can be conceived of: as a substantial and developmental opposition, enacted by representatives in the psychic apparatus, or as something perhaps even complementary, something mutually enveloping.

Freud at times appears sceptical towards the developmental optimism apparent in the metonymic scheme, and indeed it appears to go against everything psychoanalysis has discovered in the clinical field. Interestingly, when elaborating on such scepticism, the notion of narcissism seems to be Freud's central concern, such as in the 1915 edition of the *Essays*:

> Narcissistic or ego-libido seems to be the great reservoir from which the object-cathexes are sent out and into which they are withdrawn once more; the narcissistic libidinal cathexis of the ego is the original state of things, realized in earliest childhood, and is merely covered by the later extrusions of libido, but in essentials persists behind them. (1905d, p. 218)

Another story appears to lie in this concept of narcissism, and it is to this that we shall now turn.

Narcisssism and the metaphoric scheme

> Narcissism in this sense would not be a perversion, but the libidinal complement to the egoism of the instinct of self-preservation, a measure of which may justifiably be attributed to every living creature. (1914c, p. 73)

The meandering path of Freud's notion of narcissism can be traced at least from his correspondence with Jung around 1907, through the works on Leonardo and Schreber, but must be said to culminate in 1914 with *Narcissism*, which shall as such be the focus of this chapter. The text is one of Freud's most conceptually complex works, and has historically allowed for a myriad of different readings. The following discussion will focus on how this text reveals an understanding of the *I* different from the one of the metonymic scheme, situated rather in what can with Jean Laplanche be called a *metaphoric* scheme.

In *Narcissism*, to the bewilderment of the psychoanalytic community of that time (Jones, 1955, p. 302), the *I* is introduced as the fulcrum of the libido. Beyond blatantly destabilising the dualism founding the metonymic scheme, this raises the question of the subject-ego's relation to itself, of the determination and vicissitudes of the split between *I* and *me*, that is of the object-like quality of the ego. As such, it is the very notion of the paradoxical decentred centre—the Freudian dynamic par excellence—that is reintroduced in the guise of ontogenesis. Once again, as in *Dreams*, the object thought to be the base of Freud's theory, this time the adaptive *I* in ontogenesis, begins to destabilise his theory from within.

The text will be discussed stepwise, with recourse to the logical progression of the ontogenetic scheme it depicts, as illustrated in the following diagram (page numbers in brackets refer to *Narcissism*):

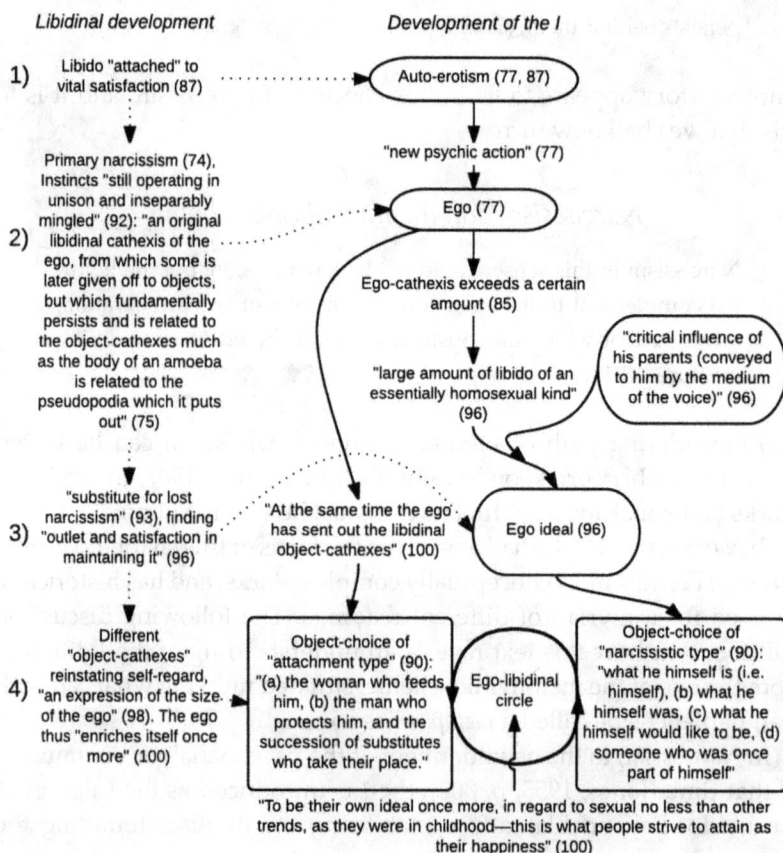

Figure 10.   1914: On Narcissism: An Introduction.

The amoeba (phases 1 and 2)

The initial stage in *Narcissism* consists simply of a definition of the libido as auto-erotically attached to means of vital satisfaction. The transition from here is most aptly stated in "Psycho-Analytic Notes on an Auto-biographical Account of a Case of Paranoia (Demential Paranoides)" (1911c) (hereafter *Psycho-analytic Notes*):

> There comes a time in the development of the individual at which he unifies his sexual instincts (which have hitherto been engaged in auto-erotic activities) in order to obtain a love-object; and he begins by taking himself, his own body, as his love-object. (p. 60)

Several things are at stake here. First of all, the drives are now said to attain an *object*, which is not auto-erotic as it implies a shift from that phase. This object is said to be a *love*-object, which already implies a relation between *totalities* (Baranger, 1991, p. 124). This may help in understanding the reintroduction of "his own body" beyond auto-erotism as something in which the subject "himself" resides. This body, then, cannot be the material body, but rather a *psychic* object defined by its totality, and by which the subject circularly comes into existence as the mirror image of itself (e.g., Lacan, 1949; Laplanche & Pontalis, 1973, p. 256). Indeed, this move is dryly said to institute the *I* as such:

> ... a unity comparable to the ego cannot exist in the individual from the start; the ego has to be developed. The auto-erotic instincts, however, are there from the very first; so there must be something added to auto-erotism—a new psychical action—in order to bring about narcissism. (Freud, 1914c, p. 77)

The nature of such "new psychical action" is nowhere specified. However, this *I* can hardly be that of adaptation, as earlier seen developed by gradual adjustment to an environment. Indeed, how could a totality be established, but all at once, by an *action*? What is clear, however, is that this *I*, this qualitatively new something that was not there before, is established at the centre of the libido, as both its subject and object, since such an action further entails:

> ... an original libidinal cathexis of the ego, from which some is later given off to objects, but which fundamentally persists and is related

to the object-cathexes much as the body of an amoeba is related to
the pseudopodia which it puts out. (ibid., p. 75)

An *I* as libidinal monad or reservoir appears absolutely incompatible
with the metonymic *I* of adaptation, and Freud's reluctant admission
as to the merely practical impossibility of differentiating the psychic
energies at this point (ibid., p. 76) cannot but be read as an attempt at
saving his dualism through obscurantism. Rather, there appears now a
metaphoric derivation of the *I* from the subject, a mirror relation disguis-
ing a qualitative difference, a relation not of homologous advocacy but
of transposition to another register.

Furthermore, such reflectivity is now explicitly tied, not to adaptation, but to a sexuality defining in *Narcissism* the entire level of psychic
differentiation. As such, one is able to make sense of the paradoxical
circularity of the subject coming into existence by falling in love with
its own body, thus constituting the subject as its own object by becoming its own *other*. The narcissistic birth of the *I* poses an insurmount-
able problem in Freud's developmental scheme because it embodies the
momentous philosophical problem of the birth of subjectivity; that is,
of the emergence of a mirror relation between the subject and itself. The
lightness with which Freud, by mere reference to some "new psychic
action", short-circuits it, however, may betray more than carelessness,
pointing towards an "always-already" of narcissism, its *fundamentality*
rather than its mere *primality*.

The *I* is now again established as centre, the earlier mentioned
"great reservoir" of the psychic apparatus, but it is a strange and passive one, the site of what is now *ego-libido*. As such, the next question
becomes: how does it become active? How does the *I* leave its homeo-
static romance with itself? Freud's explicit scheme in *Narcissism* takes
recourse to the pleasure principle, in assuming the necessity of discharg-
ing libido exceeding a certain threshold. But, as pointed out by Jean
Laplanche (1970, p. 71), since organic need has already been expelled
from the scheme, the reason for such spontaneous development of a *for
itself* out of an *in itself* is missing, rendering this explanation void.

However, as pointed out by Mikkel Borch-Jacobsen (1988, p. 53), far
from being its stumbling block, the striving to be oneself has so far been
the very motor of specific object-related desire in Freud's theory, and
this will turn out to be the case in *Narcissism* as well. Even though the
desire for the *I* appears to imply a *something* in the *I*, a substance that is

desired, the depiction of its genesis displays on the contrary the primal emptiness of the *I*, as a mere *place* in the psychic apparatus, however total, and thus in need of substantialisation by way of an other.

Narcissism thus appears essentially as something mediated, as a state or process rather than a stage. One need only recount the way in which primary narcissism in the metonymic scheme was said to be, to quote Freud in *Two Principles*, a "fiction ... however, justified when one considers that the infant—provided one includes with it the care it receives from its mother—does almost realize a psychical system of this kind" (1911b, p. 219). An explanation following the same logic now appears to make up Freud's only attempt in *Narcissism* at depicting the "psychic action" constituting the *I*, perhaps indicating the same bifurcation of understanding (cf. Borch-Jacobsen, 1988, p. 113): either primal narcissism is a fiction, or it, from the very beginning, implies object-relatedness, circularly embedded in the narcissism of the other:

> The primary narcissism of children which we have assumed ... is less easy to grasp by direct observation than to confirm by inference from elsewhere. If we look at the attitude of affectionate parents towards their children, we have to recognize that it is a revival and reproduction of their own narcissism, which they have long since abandoned. (1914c, p. 90)

Homosexuality and the ideal (phase 3)

The turning of the *I* towards objects now requires two intermediaries, homosexuality and the ideal:

> [L]arge amounts of libido of an essentially homosexual kind are drawn into the formation of the narcissistic ego ideal and find outlet and satisfaction in maintaining it. (ibid., p. 96)

The notion of dispatched ego-libido being homosexual is telling as to the object relations Freud envisions it as supporting. In order to understand why, it is necessary to return to *Psycho-analytic Notes* (1911c) in which Freud examines the seemingly non-oedipal genesis of paranoia, usually taking flight from purely social slights:

> But if we go into the matter only a little more deeply, we shall be
> able to see that the really operative factor in these social injuries
> lies in the part played in them by the homosexual components of
> emotional life … delusions never fail to uncover these relations and
> to trace back the social feelings to their roots in a directly sensual
> erotic wish. (p. 60)

Whereas usual libidinal relations can still be thought of as sexual per
se, "sublimated homosexuality" (ibid., p. 71) results rather in social
feelings, contributing "an erotic factor to friendship and comradeship,
to esprit de corps and to the love of mankind in general" (p. 61). As
pointed out by Mikkel Borch-Jacobsen (1988, p. 75), "The benefit of this
appeal to homosexuality is readily apparent. It allows the instant translation of the egoistic into the erotic, of sociality into sexuality."

However, since Freud omits any depiction of such sublimation of homosexuality, one is left with a mere insistence on ego-libido being at once social
and sexual. Freud is allowed to uphold his dualism, but at the paradoxical
cost of finding the social invisibly infected by the sexual and desexualis-
ing the ego-libido, reservoir of all libido! To quote Borch-Jacobsen again,
"[J]ust as narcissism was already a homosexual relation to oneself and as
homosexuality was still a narcissistic relation to the other (myself), sociality
is still a homosexual relation to (another) myself" (ibid., p. 87).

This homosexual ego-libido is now "drawn into the formation of the
narcissistic ego ideal" (Freud, 1914c, p. 96), the formation of which is
prompted by "the critical influence of his parents (conveyed to him by
the medium of the voice)" (p. 96) and "by which he measures his actual
ego" (p. 93). Henceforth,

> This ideal ego is now the target of the self-love which was enjoyed
> in childhood by the actual ego. … What he projects before him as
> his ideal is the substitute for the lost narcissism of his childhood in
> which he was his own ideal … and satisfaction is brought about
> from fulfilling this ideal. (ibid., p. 96)[3]

The introduction of "this new ideal ego, which, like the infantile ego,
finds itself possessed of every perfection that is of value" (ibid., p. 94) is
particularly interesting, as it seems to double the original depiction of
"primal narcissism".

Certain authors point out the way in which the *I* appears here fundamentally primal, related as subject to an ideal-as-object in an "inner

exteriority" *metonymically* modelled on an "outer exteriority" (Borch-Jacobsen, 1988, p. 94). One could argue, however, that the ideal does indeed fill out the philosophical lacks pointed out earlier, completing rather a *metaphoric* scheme. Freud introduces the ideal in an attempt to re-approach narcissism from the perspective of repression, and as such, as noted by Borch-Jacobsen (1988), it may actually be another way of stating the same thing, rather than a subsequent step in ontogenesis.

The *new psychic action* appears now explicitly to be the "critical influence of the parents", establishing for the child a displaced *vantage point* that structurally forces him into a reflective relation to himself as an object. This primal relation necessarily implies a doubling of the subject in the eyes of the desiring other (Kojève, 1969, p. 5), both of which are strictly speaking *objects*, representatives of the subject in a relation of desire: the object of parental criticism (the *I*) and its virtual measure (the ego ideal).

As such, this splitting of the *I* into two, the subject in relation to itself as object mediated by a third party, renders narcissism a fundamentally *active* process between mutually dependent parties, ouroboros chasing its tail. Since *I* and ideal are structurally differentiated objects, "primal narcissism" here becomes a *fundamentally* lost perfection, functionally a *myth* of a "pre-critical" oneness with the caregiver driving the circular movement through the ideal. The totality upon which the *I* was said to be modelled becomes the narcissistic oneness with oneself promised by the ideal. This renders conceivable why something as paradoxical as a *narcissistic object* is necessary, since the *I* must logically find objects to imitate in order to attain the ideal. Freud himself seems to point in this direction when in *Essays* he states how "The finding of an object is in fact a refinding of it" (1905d, p. 222). It is also conceivable how social desire and "homosexual" desire to be one with another oneself are logically connected.

This dynamic—between the *I*, the ideal, and the object—is what exists from this point on, pragmatically banishing primal narcissism to a mythic past (except, perhaps, in the case of psychotic megalomania (1911c, p. 65)). It is to this dynamic that we shall now turn.

Ouroboros restored: the libidinal spiral (phase 4)

> For Freud, then, love is a force that not only brings people together, one person loving another, but equally brings oneself together into that one individuality which we become through our identifications. (Gaitanidis & Curk, 2007, p. 7)

At this point, libido appears to be a unity, homogeneous within the great reservoir of the *I*. Curiously, however, having introduced the notion of the ideal, Freud adds:

> At the same time the ego has sent out the libidinal object-cathexes.
> It becomes impoverished in favour of these cathexes, just as it does
> in favour of the ego ideal, and it enriches itself once more from its
> satisfactions in respect of the object, just as it does by fulfilling its
> ideal. (1914c, p. 100)

The cause of such cathexis is nowhere specified, and one wonders how it sidesteps the ideal. A means of understanding this is by way of the name given to it later: *Anlehnungstypus* ("attachment type") (*G. W.*, *10*, p. 156; cf. 1914c, p. 87). It appears, then, to be a continuation of the way in which the drive is elsewhere said to emerge "attached" or leaning onto interactions with objects of the vital sphere, the functions of which are simply not represented in this scheme.

The notion of conflict is as such displaced from one between need and pleasure to one between two forms of pleasure, a conflict within the libido itself, between "anaclitic" and "narcissistic" object choices. These can perhaps be understood as mirroring Freud's 1908 distinction between "ambitious wishes" and "erotic wishes" (1908e, p. 147), and are enumerated thus in *Narcissism* (1914c, p. 90):

A person may love:

1. According to the narcissistic type:
a. what he himself is (i.e., himself),
b. what he himself was,
c. what he himself would like to be,
d. someone who was once part of himself.

2. According to the anaclitic (attachment) type:
a. the woman who feeds him,
b. the man who protects him.

Immediately this appears to instate a new primal dualism of the "ego-libido" and an "object-libido" (Laplanche & Pontalis, 1973, p. 151). However, as perhaps first stressed by Lou Andreas-Salomé (1921), the two choices are just as immediately drawn into the spiralling self-aspiration of the *I*, rendering them rather two *poles* of the same ego-libidinal *circuit*. Indeed, what could be more obvious than narcissism being a *mirror*-relation—what would Narcissus be, were he not locked into his own enchanted gaze? And surely, this notion is most clearly found in Freud's depiction of love, the libidinal phenomenon par excellence, in its male and female forms. In man's case:

> Complete object-love of the attachment type is, properly speaking, characteristic of the male. It displays the marked sexual overvaluation which is doubtless derived from the child's original narcissism and thus corresponds to a transference of that narcissism to the sexual object. (1914c, p. 88)

And in the case of woman:

> Strictly speaking, it is only themselves that such women love with an intensity comparable to that of the man's love for them. Nor does their need lie in the direction of loving, but of being loved; and the man who fulfils this condition is the one who finds favour with them. (ibid., p. 88)

Conclusion

What was seen implicitly in *Dreams* as "dynamic" and "structural" perspectives on the *I*, and appeared as budding in the disharmonious "anthropology" of the works preceding it, now emerges into the open as two parallel ontogenetic schemes around the notion of the drive. In thus breaking out, they appear also to break off from each other, as seen in the way in which the vital order was practically missing from the scheme in *Narcissism*. Rather, they tell each their story of what was previously taken for granted—the very place of the *I* in the psychic apparatus—with radically different implications for its substance and function.

The metonymic scheme implied an *I* as a substantially displaced representative of what one might call the subject of the organism. Its function thus became that of a representative of the outside world, of adaptation and control, a struggling autonomous agent mediating the influence of organism and environment. As such, its function naturally became defined through the *ego-instincts*, as representative of the real needs of the organism requiring satisfaction—opposed to, and attempting to tame, the libidinal drives striving solely for *pleasure*.

The metaphoric scheme epitomised in *Narcissism* on the other hand also implies an *I* of adaptation, but not that of the organism. It is an *I* of *desire*, adapted rather to the desire of the other. As such, its substance becomes that of a *place* in the psychic apparatus representing the subject as *object* for itself, structured in the gaze of the ideal, and acting as receptacle for and representative of its own worth. Rather than being opposed to the drive, the *I* is now an actor in it, partaking in its *formally* conceived aim—the reproduction of various relations to the sexual object. The function of the *I* then becomes not to attain the subject's well-being, but rather its own libidinal completion, its totalisation, and resisting attachments incompatible with this.

As in earlier chapters, the *I* is still a conqueror insisting upon being *"master in its own home"* (1917a, p. 143), and as earlier it does not realise how this desire upholds its enslavement and blindness to its own nature.

Notes

1. "… so erscheint uns der 'Trieb' als ein *Grenzbegriff* zwischen Seelischem und Somatischem, als *psychischer Repräsentant* der aus dem Körperinnern stammenden, in die *Seele* gelangenden Reize" (*G. W., 10*, p. 214, emphasis added).
2. "The defendant asserted first, that he had given it back undamaged; secondly, that the kettle had a hole in it when he borrowed it; and thirdly, that he had never borrowed a kettle from his neighbour at all" (1900a, p. 120).
3. Though later writers such as Lacan (e.g., 1977, p. 144) find a sharp conceptual distinction between ego ideal and ideal ego necessary in order to understand narcissistic dynamics, Freud himself does not seem to do so. Rather, at this point he treats them as two aspects of the same libidinal structure or tendency, with which he is concerned.

CHAPTER FOUR

The Ego and the Id: life and death on the stage of the *I*

Figure 11. *Dramatised dynamics: Narcissus approached by rejected desire in the form of Echo* (John William Waterhouse, 1903: *Echo and Narcissus*).

Preface

In *The Ego and the Id* (1923b) (henceforth *Ego and Id*) Freud introduces his "second topography", popularly known as the "structural model", in a self-proclaimed attempt to further develop "some trains of thought which I opened up in *Beyond the Pleasure Principle*" (henceforth *Beyond*) (1923b, p. 12). As argued by James Strachey, *Ego and Id* is possibly "the last of Freud's major theoretical works" (1923b, p. 4). As such, it shall in this chapter represent the last phase of Freud's conceptualisation of the *I*, spanning the works from *Beyond* to the posthumously published *An Outline of Psycho-Analysis* of 1938 (1940a).

In his new model, Freud projects dynamic assemblages or "systems" (Schmidt-Hellerau, 2001, p. 210), ego—id—superego, onto the *Pcpt.-Cs.—Pcs.—Ucs.* triad of the first topography. This shifts Freud's theoretical focus from "where" a representation is active to where "effective control" resides (Hill, 1980, p. 340):[1]

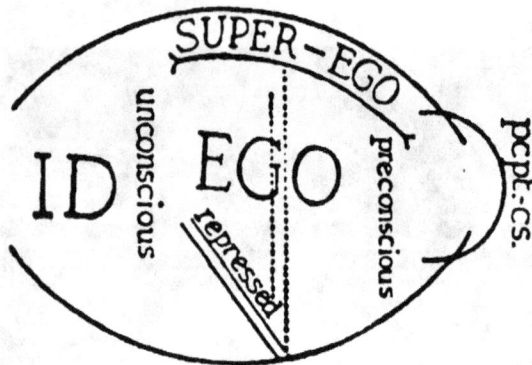

Figure 12. The structural model.

As Strachey (Freud, 1923b, p. 10) further notes, "It is as an equivalent to the 'ego ideal' that '*das Über-Ich*' [the superego, literally 'over-I'] makes its first appearance" in 1923, and in the following it shall be treated as a continuation of this notion such as previously elaborated in *Narcissism* (1914c). The id (*das Es* (G. W., 13, p. 237)—literally "the it"), however, is a new term, defined repeatedly as a "something" into which the *I* extends (e.g., 1923b, p. 23), and "which contains the passions" (p. 25). Both id and superego will be discussed at length as they relate to and thus redefine the *I* in this phase of Freud's work.

In introducing this new model, *Ego and Id* reads like a general revision, a patchwork of earlier thoughts, its footnotes (including Strachey's) referring to no less than fourteen volumes of the *Standard Edition*. It is therefore necessary in the following to appraise the text in two aspects: first in its formal aspect—what are the consequences of the inscription of the *I* into the second topography? And second, in its substantial and dynamic aspects—what is the actual "content" of the *I* as elaborated in this phase?

With respect to the *formal* aspect, the central trait will turn out to be the text's depiction of psychical dynamics through anthropomorphic language (Laplanche, 1999b, p. 141) and wide-ranging use of metaphor (Montgomery, 2001), revealing what seems to be an autonomisation of the *I* as essentially a *dramatisation*. This was found earlier in Freud's depictions of the wish played out in dreams and the drive as structure or "act", implying active relations based on, or mirroring, static structures, and it is exactly such notions that re-emerge within what will turn out to be essentially the conception of the *I* of *Narcissism*.

In that work of 1914, narcissism was depicted as a cycle of psychical *life*, tending to homogenise the psychic apparatus by monopolising the libido as essentially an ego-libido. As pointed out by Ahmed Fayek (1981), however, the theme of *death* is centrally present in the myth of Narcissus—and, one might add, doubly so: first as repetitive, incompatible, and rejected desire in the form of Echo, second as Narcissus's deathly fixation upon his own image. In this chapter it shall be argued that, with respect to its *content*, what is new in *Ego and Id* is such a return, in the midst of narcissistic homeostasis, of the drive in its transgressive, radical moment, as a servant of death. The Freudian *I* now finds its last form structured between the narcissistic circuit of the superego and a new one defined by the id.

General implications of the second topography

Despite *Ego and Id*'s complexity, prominent commentators agree in stressing a tendency towards duality in its depiction of the *I*, whereby seemingly conflicting characteristics are, once again, seamlessly interwoven. A commonly stressed duality is one between what Bruce Fink (2004, p. 41) calls *structure* and *agency*. Simo Køppe and O. A. Olsen (1983, p. 157) appear to indicate the same in their distinction between the *I* as having a functional as well as an identificatory core. Another group depict the *I* as split between *heteronomy* and *independence* (e.g., Laplanche & Pontalis, 1973, p. 139), being simultaneously *agent of adaptation* and *defence* (Hill, 1980, p. 347).

In his introduction, James Strachey notes that in *Ego and Id*, Freud returns to the nature of the *I* of *Entwurf* (1923b, p. 4). In keeping with this, I would argue that the first set of dualities can be read as what was, in the discussion of this text, separated as *functional* and *substantial* aspects of the *I*—that is, roughly, what the *I does* and what it *consists of*, respectively. The other set, I would again argue, essentially indicates the addition of an *agentic* aspect.

The functional aspect of the I

With respect to its *functional* depiction, it is now said that the "nucleus" of the *I* is "the system Pcpt." (ibid., p. 23), rendering it "the representative of the external world, of reality" (p. 36), and "what may be called reason and common sense" (p. 25). It is as such "entrusted with important functions. … it gives mental processes an order in time and submits them to 'reality-testing'. By interposing the processes of thinking, it secures a postponement of motor discharges and controls the access to motility" (p. 55). In this aspect, then, the *I* appears to embody an undisturbed echo of the earlier reality-ego (Køppe & Olsen, 1983, p. 161), with the addition of what may be called an *agentic* touch.

The substantial aspect of the I

Substantially too, the *I* is notably reminiscent of that of the earliest phase of Freud's work. Rather than a reified centre of agency, the *I* is depicted as a generic centre of psychic *stability* by which certain functions are made possible: "We have formed the idea that in each individual there is a coherent organisation of mental processes; and we call this his *ego*" (1923b, p. 17). As also was the case earlier, such as in the structural perspective in *Dreams*, it is now said that resistance merely "emanates from" (p. 18) the *I*, as an effect of "the antithesis between the coherent ego and the repressed which is split off from it" (p. 17). Such representational substance is further combined with its genetic mechanism that was earlier seen in *Narcissism*. Most centrally, it is stated that:

> When it happens that a person has to give up a sexual object, there quite often ensues an alteration of his ego which can only be described as a setting up of the object inside the ego, as it occurs in melancholia … the process, especially in the early phases of development, is a very frequent one, and it makes it possible to suppose that the character of the ego is a precipitate of abandoned object-cathexes and that it contains the history of those object-choices. (ibid., p. 29)

As noted by Silvia Halperin and C. S. Shakow (1989, p. 369), Freud thus generalises "the model of narcissistic identification" into "a fundamental mechanism in the structuring of the ego".

The I as intrapsychic agent

But the *I* is depicted with an intrapsychic face as well, in which it distances itself from adaptive functionality, all the while retaining its agentic aspect. Here, we read, the *I*:

> … tries to remain on good terms with the id; it clothes the id's *Ucs.* commands with its *Pcs.* rationalizations; it pretends that the id is showing obedience to the admonitions of reality, even when in fact it is remaining obstinate and unyielding; it disguises the id's conflicts with reality and, if possible, its conflicts with the super-ego too. In its position midway between the id and reality, it only too often yields to the temptation to become sycophantic, opportunist and lying, like a politician who sees the truth but wants to keep his place in popular favour. (1923b, p. 56)

The *I pretends*, it *disguises*, it *yields to temptation*. Is this still the adaptive, functional reality-ego? As noted by Scott Montgomery (2001, p. 69), having utilised a language of science and machinery for the depiction of the *I* in its external relations, Freud unnoticeably slips into a language of passion as soon as he touches upon the *I* in its internal relations. In its relations to the id, a very bodily, very inconvenient *I* is suddenly found riding a wild horse (1923b, p. 25), or seductively attempting to convince the id that "Look, you can love me too" (p. 30). As the superego enters the stage, metaphors of fate (p. 57), natural history (p. 35), political intrigue (p. 55), and finally *war* enter with it: while undertaking its "conquest of the id … [the *I*'s] struggle against the libido exposes it to the danger of maltreatment and death … suffering under the attacks of the super-ego or perhaps even succumbing to them" (p. 56). Surely now, the agentic definition of the *I* is not easily reduced to the functional *I* as reality-ego or aspects of its substance, but seems rather to indicate a third aspect of its depiction.

Agency as a third term

Certain authors (e.g., Hartmann, Kris, & Loewenstein, 1946) have used this occasion to read *Ego and Id* as introducing an intrapsychic *I* of adaptation, rather than the passively adaptive functional *I* of *Entwurf*. And surely, the agentic discourse of the text appears to transpose a conscious "psychological" *I* of a vital adaptive register, the metonymic scheme, back into the objectal realm of intrapsychic structure.

Others, however, warn against taking such anthropomorphisation at face value (Køppe & Olsen, 1983, p. 158). Rather, it can be argued that this narrative slippage into psychic phenomenology can be understood by noticing how Freud, while animating his new entities, refers to a "*seelische Dynamik*" (G. W., 13, p. 240) or "*seelische Vorgänge*" which are not necessarily conscious (Montgomery, 2001). Indeed, Freud explicitly establishes the differentiation between *I*, id and superego as a "*Gliederung des seelischen Wesens*" (G. W., 13, p. 268), differentiations in *psychical being*, and not the "*Apparat*" as such. The latter term still appears reserved for references to aspects of his first topography, such as consciousness (p. 246) or perception (p. 249). As noted by Scott Montgomery (2001, p. 56), dynamics in physics refer to causes, that is forces and mechanisms rather than substances. The animism by which the *I* for instance "feels itself hated and persecuted by the super-ego" (1923b, p. 58), can as such be read as similar to that by which two magnets "feel attracted to each other". Read thus, the agencies of *Ego and Id* would refer to dynamic aspects or processes of the unconscious, rather than substances.

Agency as dramatisation

In its substance, then, the *I* of *Ego and Id* arguably takes up the thread running through the substantial definition of the *I* in *Entwurf*, the structural definition in *Dreams*, and the metaphoric scheme of *Narcissism*. In the words of Laplanche and Pontalis (1973, p. 142), such *I* is not in itself a centre of rational agency, but essentially "an internal formation originating from *certain privileged perceptions* which derive not from the external world in general, but specifically from the interhuman world".

Bernard Apfelbaum (1966, p. 465) goes so far as to argue that Freud in *Ego and Id* "makes it clear that this ego of common sense is not his concern". Rather, his explicit interest should be seen as the *I insofar as it is unconscious*, structured in unconscious dynamics. Such a reading surely is not without justification. As Freud states early in *Ego and Id*: "We should like to learn more about the ego, now that we know that it, too, can be unconscious in the proper sense of the word" (1923b, p. 19). The struggles of the *I*, then, appear not so much to be an expression of weakness as one of continuity with the element of the unconscious (Apfelbaum, 1966, p. 456).

At the same time, *Ego and Id* clearly establishes the *I* as centre of the adaptive functions it was ascribed in earlier works. In keeping with this duality, the *I* is now in a central passage said to be "first and foremost a bodily ego; it is not merely a surface entity, but is itself the projection of a surface" (1923b, p. 26). This compact formulation arguably implies the doubling of the *I* found in previous works, but now with both present in the same place: the *I* as "surface entity", that is as a differentiated "cortical layer" (ibid., p. 26), a reality ego with *Pcpt.* as its nucleus, mirroring an *I* as internalisation of the body-totality, its "nucleus" being rather the internalised other, evolving by the mechanism of identification. That this is an actual doubling is confirmed in a footnote of 1927: "It may thus be regarded as a mental projection of the surface of the body, besides, as we have seen above, representing the superficies of the mental apparatus" (p. 26). Such doubling in one place, it may be argued, had already been underway for quite some time, as is seen for instance in the largely parallel flow charts of *Vicissitudes* and *Narcissism*. To my knowledge, however, it is not until this point that they are so explicitly connected:

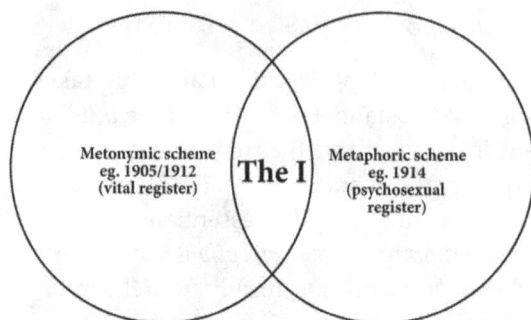

Figure 13. The *I* as intersection between the metaphoric and metonymic *schemes.*

When inner conflicts are depicted as influencing what appears as an outwardly active double of the *I*, this can now be read as an implication of such parallelisation of the metonymic and metaphoric schemes, rendering the beloved substantial *I* "the link necessary in man, for him to be able to struggle to keep himself alive" (Laplanche, 1999b, p. 176). Such reading, I would further argue, is fully in keeping with *Beyond*, which *Ego and Id* is supposed to be a development of, and in which Freud establishes the aim of both within a common principle, the life drive Eros:

> [I]t is all the more necessary for us to lay stress upon the libidinal character of the self-preservative instincts now that we are venturing upon the further step of recognizing the sexual instinct as Eros, the preserver of all things, and of deriving the narcissistic libido of the ego from the stores of libido by means of which the cells of the soma are attached to one another. (1920g, p. 52)

Structure as stasis

Freud himself explains the introduction of his new model as a consequence of his discovery that the *I*'s defences against the id's drives are unconscious, blurring the categorical differentiations between *Pcs.* and *Ucs.* (1923b, p. 17). However, "discoveries" of how "symptoms arose through the psychical mechanism of (unconscious) *defence*" (1896b, p. 162), such as in this quote from "Further remarks on the neuropsychoses of defence" of 1896, have been present in Freud's writings all along. Jean Laplanche (1999b, p. 136) notes that such re-ascription of an unconscious defensive function to the *I* must be read as a continuation of the more recent discovery of the overdetermination of the *I* in *phantasy*, that is, the "imaginary scene in which the subject is a protagonist, representing the fulfilment of a wish" (Laplanche & Pontalis, 1973, p. 314).

A telling example of this is found in Freud's *A Child Is Being Beaten* of 1919, named after the conscious phantasy of the protagonist. Her unconscious phantasy, however, reads "'I am being beaten by my father' ... But we may say of it in a certain sense that it has never had a real existence. It is never remembered, it has never succeeded in becoming conscious" (1919e, p. 185). The phantasy, so to speak, *insists* in the patient's experience, rather than *existing* as an object of it. In the text, the phantasy's scene is moulded by the Oedipus complex; that is, as will be seen later, as a compromise between desire and idealisation—the id and the superego— implicitly structuring the dynamics of the unconscious as they unfold in time. This is, roughly, what was earlier implied by the drive as act rather than impulse (Fayek, 2013, p. 155), allowing a *structural* reading, vis-á-vis *Dreams*, of the interactions of the three agencies, rendering such interactions dramatisations of a common script immanent in the negotiations between what appear to be autonomous actors. While diachronically their interactions seem concerned with particular approaching contents and reactions, synchronically these appear now as structured in phantasy as an implicit scene defining the characters enacted by the agencies. As such, the intersection of id and superego in the *I*, to be elaborated further on, mirrors

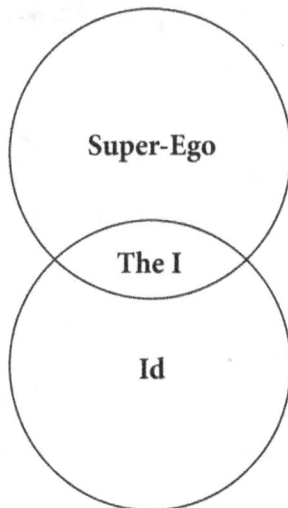

Figure 14. The *I* as intersection between id and superego.

the point of intersection noted in *Dreams* where the *Ucs.* was located as an immanent structure or scene in the very texture of intrapsychic dynamics:

In summary, the *I* of *Ego and Id* figures within a double intersection between metonymic and metaphoric schemes and the id and superego, acting as a dynamic centre of both pairs, and as a structuring centre of passage across these dualities, which can now be merged into one schema:

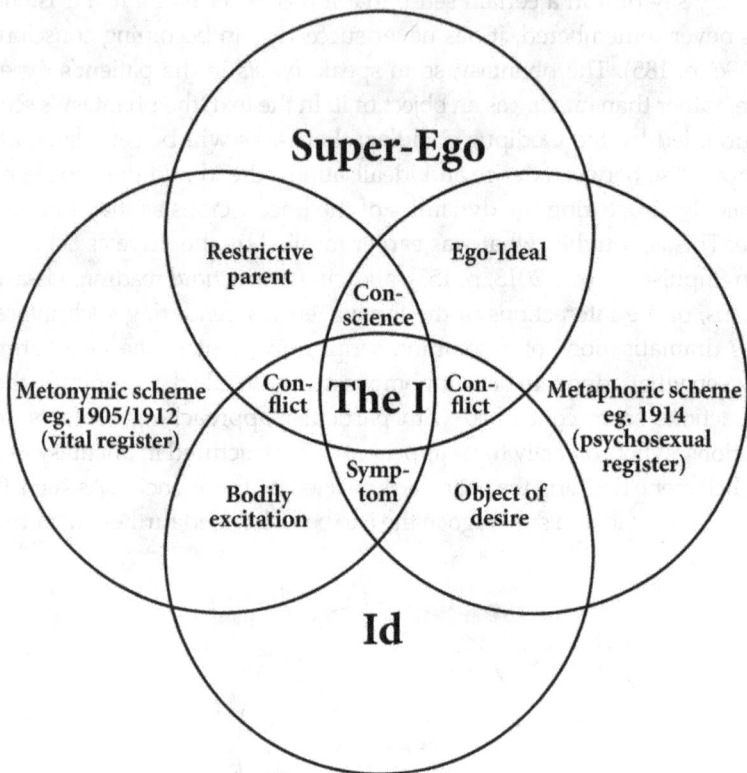

Figure 15. The *I* as dynamic centre of Freud's theory.

On the one hand, then, the model above indicates the parameters of the *synchronic* structure, the unconscious phantasy defined as a driving script, in the intersection between id and superego. On the other, it further allows for a more tangible grasp of the *I* in its *diachronic* aspect, where it is seen how the id and superego embody principles of libidinal flows in time, centred on the *I*. Since the nature of the unconscious as structure has to some extent been dealt with earlier—in phantasy, the drive as act, and the dream as expression of a properly unconscious wish—it is to this latter reading of the model that we shall now turn. In this aspect, the agentic narrative of the *I* complementary to its structural depiction is reintroduced, completing yet another rendition of the dual *I* with which we are by now familiar. This time, though, both are seemingly set within the libidinal sphere established with the metaphoric scheme of the previous chapter, merely attached to, or with implications for, the adaptive functions of the organism. In order to shed light on such flows and progressively unfold the model as it applies to these, it is necessary to consider the *I* as defined in its relations to the superego and id respectively.

The I *as defined in its relation to the superego*

As noted, Freud appears in *Ego and Id* to use the terms "super-ego" and "ego ideal" interchangeably. Indeed, such admixing is undertaken with open eyes, as in the title of the chapter in which the nature of the super-ego is elaborated, exactly through its relation to the *I*: "The Ego and the Super-ego (Ego Ideal)" (1923b, p. 28).

In *Narcissism* the *I*'s relation to the ego ideal was clearly defined as an idealising narcissistic libidinal circuit. Why does Freud now introduce the term superego if it is simply to be read as the equivalent of the ego ideal? Should the term ego ideal not have been abandoned altogether, were it merely a consequence of the dramatised perspective of *Ego and Id*? I would argue that the key to this question is to be found in Freud's notion of how the superego per se is "heir to the Oedipus complex" (1923b, p. 48), indicating a *consequence* rather than a beginning, and thus an addition to the primary, even primal, nature of the ego ideal and its circuit. In *Narcissism*, the "content" of the ideal was left undefined—this, I would argue, is exactly the gap that the superego fills out.

The Oedipus complex

The oedipal drama in *Ego and Id* begins with a state structured by the presence of "two psychologically distinct ties" (1921c, p. 105) defined as the *I*'s *having* and *being* the desired object (p. 106):

> At a very early age the little boy develops an object-cathexis for his mother, which originally related to the mother's breast and is the prototype of an object-choice on the anaclitic model; the boy deals with his father by identifying himself with him. (1923b, p. 31)

Already, then, the narrative has distanced itself from the notion of the ego ideal, insofar as this was taken, in instigating the *I* as total object, to be a *precondition* for the cathexis of the total mother. As noted by Mikkel Borch-Jacobsen (1988, p. 176), Freud had already, in *Group Psychology and the Analysis of the Ego* (1921c), been operating with two notions of such primal identification. Besides the one parallel with the cathexis of the mother, in *Ego and Id* it is said that the superego is "the first identification and one which took place while the ego was still feeble" (1923b, p. 48). This notion of primal identification appears to mirror that of *Narcissism*, as confirmed when Freud projects its origin backwards into a pre-subjective oral phase (1921c, p. 105). In *Ego and Id*, however, Freud's focus is identification insofar as it is *parallel* to object-cathexis—not in its instating, primal moment, but rather insofar as it points forward towards the Oedipus complex.

Freud continues by describing how the desire for the mother is intensified, making a rival of the father (1923b, p. 32). Due to a constitutional bisexuality (p. 31) of a nature too complex to be depicted here, the consequence of such conflict is, in the boy's case, a strengthened identification with the father and an abandonment of the cathexis of the mother, combined with some measure of identification with her (p. 34). The prohibition of incest comes to disguise the incapacity for incest, motivating a fixation on the figure of the father as a key to narcissistic unity with the mother (Chasseguet-Smirgel & Grunberger, 1986, p. 42). The general outcome of this phase is now:

> ... the forming of a precipitate in the ego, consisting of these two identifications [with both parents] *in some way united with each other. This modification of the ego retains its special position; it confronts the other contents of the ego as an ego ideal or super-ego.* (1923b, p. 34)

The oedipal aspect of the ego ideal, the superego per se, is now defined as an identification residing in the *I* itself, defining the face of the ego ideal. As such, Freud depicts the superego, not as a generic ideal, but rather one as animated through the confrontation with the actual parents, resulting in an inner voice of *conscience* (ibid., p. 37). What now is the nature of such a voice?

> The super-ego is, however, not simply a residue of the earliest object-choices of the id [primal identification as oral incorporation];

> it also represents an energetic reaction-formation against those
> choices [in the Oedipus complex]. Its relation to the ego is not
> exhausted by the precept: "You *ought to be* like this (like your
> father)." It also comprises the prohibition: "You *may not be* like this
> (like your father)—that is, you may not do all that he does; some
> things are his prerogative." (ibid., p. 34)

You may *not*—rather than an internalisation of the pure voice of the parents, the ego ideal as superego becomes a representative of the *relation* to the parents (ibid., p. 36). Beyond a mere voice of alienation, "Be like me," it is now also a voice of *separation*, as defining a detached desire of the parental Other that actively separates the *I* from its sought narcissistic oneness with the ideal. However, this is a voice of *prohibition* as well, establishing a border against the imitation of this desire itself—in the boy's case, the desire for the mother. This should come as no surprise, since the intrapsychic nature of the drive as activity or "scene" means that *having* the object implies a *being*—in this case a being too closely resembling the father's. Such perpetually conflictual reunion of desire as being and having can now be seen as the very essence of the Oedipus complex (Borch-Jacobsen, 1988, p. 220).

In summary, the superego now diachronically acts as a structure defining an intrapsychic libidinal circuit upholding a definition of the *I* within the bounds of the parental (paternal) ideal.

The I as defined in its relation to the id

Just as it was necessary to understand the superego in its structuring function within a drive circuit with the *I*, so the id must be understood in a similar circuit with the *I*, this time defined by the concept of the *death drive* and, as it turns out, a notion of nature (Dufresne, 2000; Tomlinson, 2011). In a central passage on the id, it is stated that:

> Eros and the death instinct struggle within it … It would be possible to picture the id as under the domination of the mute but powerful death instincts, which desire to be at peace and (prompted by the pleasure principle) to put Eros, the mischief-maker, to rest. (1923b, p. 59)

Eros, the life drive—the id tends to oppose itself to it, and in a quite particular way, which we read in a footnote paying homage to the author of the concept, Georg Groddeck, while implying Freud's fidelity to its original rendition:

> Groddeck himself no doubt followed the example of Nietzsche, who habitually used this grammatical term for whatever in our nature is impersonal and, so to speak, subject to natural law. (ibid., p. 23)

Impersonal, subject to natural law, and opposed to the life drive. With this in mind, in order to understand the nature of the id, a detour around the dualism of death- and life-drives is necessary.

The mechanism and aim of the death drive

> Physiologists should think twice before positioning the drive for self-preservation as the cardinal drive of an organic being. Above all, a living thing wants to *discharge* its strength. (Friedrich Nietzsche, 2001, §13)

Historically, the death drive has been the enfant terrible of psychoanalysis (e.g., Akhtar & O'Neil, 2011, p. 2). Certain authors, however, stress how the death drive, rather than being something radically new, is the continuation of several themes left unfinished in Freud's theorisation, going back as far as *Entwurf* (Caropreso & Simanke, 2008, p. 87).

Recall how in *Entwurf* Freud's principal dynamic of the psychic apparatus was *inertia*, a tendency towards total discharge of free energy, defining the "primary principle". Its obverse was the principle of constancy, and pleasure was established somewhere in between, in the process of discharge of energy, unpleasure in its accumulation. The primary opposition, then, was between inertia and constancy, not inertia and pleasure. The notion of constancy was from the beginning connected to the notion of binding, defining the *I* as a constant structure in the psychic apparatus. This was further attached to consciousness, and hence the qualitative level on which pleasure per se must be said to reside (Køppe & Olsen, 1981, p. 346).

In *Beyond* where the death drive is introduced, Freud now specifies the nature of the drive in general by two notions. First, it is said to be compulsively *repetitive* (1920g, p. 36). Second, it is essentially *conservative* as moving by a "backward path that leads to complete satisfaction" (p. 42).

In light of earlier expositions, I would argue that this now implicitly re-establishes two notions of pleasure, two logics of the drive, which were earlier seen attached to the metonymic and metaphoric schemes, now overlapping in the *I*. If pleasure is thought of *functionally* as discharge, it tends towards reproducing the state before accumulation of tension, and thus essentially implies a movement towards zero tension, *antagonising* the *I* as constant cathexis: "*the aim of all life is death*" (ibid., p. 38). If, however, pleasure is thought of *structurally*, as within the metaphoric psychosexual register, the bottom level of tension is that of the structure itself, implying a movement towards repetition of the scene of satisfaction understood as primal erotogenic stimulation (Laplanche, 1987, p. 153), or narcissistic structuration *sustaining* the *I*. Furthermore, the starting point of the metonymic scheme was the biological organism, logically preceded by inorganic matter. The starting point of the metaphoric scheme, on the other hand, was psychical life, its preceding state a myth. This notion is repeated in *Beyond* (1920g, p. 57) in which the state towards which the drive as life drive, that is, as bound by the structure of the *I*, strives, is the totality of Aristophanes' myth in Plato's *Symposium*.[2]

As argued by Gunnar Karlsson (1998), the "inorganic state" can now be read as its analogy in mental life: the dissolution, the unbinding, of the *I*, keeping both life- and death drives within a metaphoric scheme. Others such as Todd Dufresne (2000, p. 143), however, insist that the "organic" aspect of the death drive in Freud's depiction should not be rejected offhandedly, since the redefinition of free energy as essentially a death drive concerns the organism as a whole (Caropreso & Simanke, 2008, p. 89).

On a *microscopic* level, the drive, Freud says, reveals itself in the fact of certain microorganisms dying when left in their own waste products, but not those of others (1920g, p. 48). On a *macroscopic* level, the repetitive nature of the drive is exemplified by the migration patterns of certain fishes and birds of passage, implying an "organic compulsion to repeat" (p. 37). As an almost cosmic principle, the drive as death drive appears now to be the very course of nature in psychical life, a *natural law* that in its blind repetitiveness is indifferent to life— a nature that spills over into the psychical sphere, or a part of psychical life regressing into a natural process. As noted by Todd Dufresne (2000, p. 140), in Freud's early works, self-preservation as the stabilising tendency of vital life was disrupted by the psychical force of sexuality. The tables have now turned, as sexuality in its organic aspect is here what disrupts a psychical core of life.

What appears now "beyond the pleasure principle", beyond the *I* as structure, is a *death drive*, insofar as the energy thus discharged is the stuff of life (Lind, 1991, p. 77). As put by Jean-Bertrand Pontalis (in Lacan, 1988, p. 23), it is the drive in its mechanical moment, detached from any constructively determined aim, embodying a pleasure principle in its purest, most radical form. Here, within the bounds of the psychic apparatus, a tendency towards discharge paying no heed to constancy, reality, or life itself reappears, driving the organism towards zero tension beyond the grasp of the *I*.

The id as libidinal circuit

The tendency to unbinding, a catabolisation of intrapsychic structure and with it extrapsychic adaptability, that now characterises the death drive is, I would argue, throughout the works of the early 1920s seen particularly clearly under two conditions, both defined by the nature of the *I*. One is found in a peculiar tendency to narcissistic hostility against peers and "*nahestehende Fremde*" (G. W., 13, p. 111—"close strangers", seemingly a pun upon "close friends"), to which one had earlier enjoyed a brotherly bond, when they transgress against the ideal or strive to approximate it at the group's expense (1920g, p. 120). The other is found in the tendency of the id for discharge through a libidinal circuit independent of the narcissistic one, incompatible with integration into the narcissistic structure. Such conditions can now furthermore be read as defined by the two commandments of the superego, as the *I* meets its limit both too close to and too far from its ideal. As such, what is found in both spaces is still "tinged with erotism" (Laplanche & Pontalis, 1973, p. 99), desires of a single libidinal type (Laplanche, 2004), but both defined by being incompatible with the *I* as structure and both counteracting it. Just as a primal state ruled by the primary process was established as myth, the death drive of the second topography is still teleologically defined by the life drive (Schmidt-Hellerau, 2001, p. 186). Of special interest now are the id and the circuit of the drive defining its relation to the *I*.

First of all, in contrast to *Narcissism*, we are told that the function of the great reservoir of the libido is now ascribed to the id (1923b, p. 30). As such, the circuit of the id is established as potentially separate from that of the ego ideal:

> [O]bject-cathexes proceed from the id, which feels erotic trends as needs. The ego, which to begin with is still feeble, becomes aware of the object-cathexes, and either acquiesces in them or tries to fend them off by the process of repression. ... It may be that this identification is the sole condition under which the id can give up its objects. (p. 29)

Such object-cathexes are now immediately identifiable as those said in *Narcissism* to be sent out "at the same time" as their narcissistic counterparts, the drives of *Essays* proper, now originally separate from narcissism. As noted by André Green, what then returns in the id as such, is simply the drives (2001, p. 66). Furthermore, it is noted that these are now, if not bound in the narcissistic circuit, fended off by the *I*, and we may add—in keeping with the first commandment of the superego. As an approaching drive implying a certain being of the *I*, the id now earns its name of an *it* striving to become an *I*, a "something in me at that moment that was stronger than me" (1926e, p. 195).

As stated earlier, this rejection from the integration into the *I* as identification is at the same time a rejection from the secondary process, forcing the object-libido to follow a pattern of discharge further counteracting the stability of the *I*, and in light of the aforementioned parallel schemes, in its organic as well as intrapsychically self-preserving aspect. Here, then, is where the libido of the id-circuit begins its development into a death drive proper. This is understandable when remembering how such a process of "repression" was in *Studies* said to lead the libido towards *bodily* representations. Such a regression, however, is now still established on the basis of an intrapsychically defined desire, and so, as put by Bruce Fink (1995, p. 114), "[T]he medium the symptoms adopt is ... a body overwritten with signifiers"; that is, by the substance of psychic organisation.

In summary then, the id acts as a structure defining an intrapsychic libidinal circuit, starting in a desired having of the object, implying a being of the *I*, and resulting in a symptomatic re-immersion into the body. It stands in contrast to the circuit of the *I* and superego, upholding stability but also a kind of self-enclosed libidinal stasis. In both circuits, the *I* is the defining centrepiece, mediating also the influence of libidinal energy on the organic sphere, whether in the form of law-abiding stability or symptomatic disruption. In place of further summary, however, we shall now jump straight to a general review of the readings undertaken, in order to finally show how Freud in this most complicated text has in fact simply incorporated most aspects of the *I* elaborated so far into a whole.

Retrospective

Figure 16. World egg containing the Rebis, doubled subject, below it the dragon of chaos, above the realm of the Law.

Looking back upon the preceding discussions, one aspect of the Freudian *I* appears particularly central: its persistent paradoxical double nature, consisting of two simultaneous viewpoints—that of its own perspective and that of the sites of the unconscious in the respective phases of Freud's writings.

From the perspective of the *I* itself, what appears as a reified "psychological" *I as subject* is depicted as driven by relatively independent motives of its own: an active *I* as agent of higher psychological functions, social adaptation, mental censorship, self-preservation, and oedipal subservience. Generally, this perspective implies a diachronic and thus dynamic vision of the *I*, whereby the determinants of its substance structuring its motives tend to disappear from sight.

From what may tentatively be called a "perspective of the unconscious", an *I as object* appears as a piece in a synchronic *meta*psychological mechanism or structure, defining the very substance by which the *I* is able to appear motivated: a structure defined around social positions, infantile wishes, narcissistic idealisations, and oedipal phantasies. Hereby, however, the unfolding functions and phenomenological aspect of the *I*, frozen in a synchronic image, tend to disappear from sight.

Going into further detail, in the first chapter, the *I* of *Studies* and *Entwurf* was depicted as an intrapsychic representative of the subject, a nucleus of socially acceptable representations defining its own incompatible unconscious counterpart. The *I* as *subject* was seen to be a defensive agent of higher psychological functions and inner as well as outer stability, keeping incompatible impulses at bay, implying the possibility of relief by decoding their symptomatic materialisations. On the other hand, the *I* also acted as an intrapsychic *object*, a core of preferred representations, the nature of which was seen to be the actual cause of its own suffering. Such perspective seemed to imply the inverse necessity of unfolding the substance of the *I* in order for the suffering subject to come to terms with the structural cause of its malady—moral weakness.

In the second chapter, the *I* of *Dreams* appeared without its externally adaptive guise, posing as a "pleasure-seeking" agency operating on what appeared to be different psychic levels. Social structure had here left the outside world, only to slip in between the lines of the dream-text. The *I* as *subject* was again a defensive agent, now explicitly striving to uphold its own consistency against the pressure of latent impulses, allowing for a therapeutic decoding of these in the manifest dream-text as the central means of insight into the psyche. On the other hand, the *I* was seen to be structured as an *object* in an unconscious wish overdetermining the very translation from latent to manifest, which would then be the proper object of interpretation, in order for the subject to come to terms with itself.

In the third chapter, the *I* of especially *Essays* and *Narcissism* was even further involved in either a struggle or an osmosis with the drive on a perhaps even more abstract ontogenetic level. The *I* as *subject* was depicted as a vitally adaptive agency, struggling with drives as impulsive urges. This implied the possibility of a reciprocal adaptation of self-preserving and sexual needs in the development towards genital sexuality. On the other hand, the *I* as *object* was itself an entity of the psychosexual sphere, striving for stasis and completion rather than development, itself a structuring centre of the drives and thus implying the necessity of analysing the *I*'s narcissistic attachment to its own ideal image on any path to structural change.

In the fourth chapter, the *I* of *Ego and Id* appeared to integrate the previous *I*'s of psychopathology, common unconscious formations, and ontogenesis into one scheme with a diachronic and a synchronic side, corresponding well to the two sides of the *I* such as elaborated so far. An *I* as *subject* appeared here within a *diachronic* process as the intrapsychic turning point of the total organism's relation to itself, caught between object-oriented desires and parental law. On the other hand, the *I* was itself an *object* in a static, *synchronic*, "phantasmatic" fixation of a relation between id and superego, making the uncovering of a structuring fundamental phantasy a deeper aim of analysis than focusing on particular aspects of the law of the superego or urges of the id. As an integrative model, we are now further in a position to notice how Freud with *Ego and Id* has undertaken a circle back to his earliest conceptualisations of the *I*, reactivating insights from his entire work in one whole.

First, the notions of a substantial and functional *I* of *Entwurf* live on in two parallel sides of the *I* of *Ego and Id*, both covered by a layer of agentic discourse. Besides this, the "pathogenic nucleus" of *Studies* finds its equal in the id as rejected desire returning in the body, incompatible with the substance of the *I*, now defined within the narcissistic circuit with the superego's moral law.

The structural perspective of *Dreams* is present as integrated into the structure of the intersection between id and superego defining the motivation of the *I*. Its dynamic perspective is present in the diachronic outlook of this *I*, caught in a continual struggle between having and being, desire and idealisation, resulting in distorted manifest expressions of various impulses.

And finally, as elaborated at length, both metonymic and metaphoric schemes of the *I* as the object of extrapsychic adaptation and intrapsychic integration respectively are simultaneously present around the *I* as the point that connects these two dimensions.

When introducing his new model in *Ego and Id*, Freud himself likens it to *an egg* (1923b, p. 24) and we may now add, a *world egg* in which the divinities reside. On a final note, this suggestive metaphor for the model that apparently weaves together Freud's entire vision of the *I*, and this survey with it, can perhaps be unfolded through the words of Gilles Deleuze:

> The world is an egg, but the egg itself is a theatre: a staged theatre in which the roles dominate the actors, the spaces dominate the roles and the Ideas dominate the spaces. (1994, p. 281)

Thus viewed, what is the second topography if not the depiction of a dynamic breeding ground of intrapsychic phenomena, their *theatre itself*? What are its agencies if not the spaces, as of an equation, thought to structure any role, any identification taken up by the acting subject? And finally, what is the act itself if not a reification of the nature of the drive as drama, circling around an unconscious as question, as problematic, the inaugural Idea?[3]

Notes

1. For the sake of simplicity, this is the more developed model of *New Introductory Lectures on Psycho-Analysis* (1933a, p. 78), differing from the version of *Ego and Id* (1923b, p. 24) in two aspects only: first of all, the model is now "open at its end to somatic influences" (1933a, p. 73). Second, the superego has replaced the so-called "cap of hearing" (1923b, p. 25), substantiating the relation between the voice of the parents and the superego/ego ideal indicated in the previous chapter.
2. This is the theory which Plato put into the mouth of Aristophanes in the *Symposium*, and which deals not only with the *origin* of the sexual instinct but also with the most important of its variations in relation to its object. "The original human nature was not like the present, but different. In the first place, the sexes were originally three in number, not two as they are now; there was man, woman, and the union of the two." Everything about these primaeval men was double: they had four hands and four feet, two faces, two privy parts, and so on. Eventually Zeus decided to cut these men in two, "like a sorb-apple which is halved for pickling". After the division had been

made, "… the two parts of man, each desiring his other half, came together, and threw their arms about one another eager to grow into one" (1920g, p. 57).

3. Deleuze and Guattari (1977, p. 24) bemoan how psychoanalysis turns this stage into a factory, fixating a certain play on it and reifying this in focusing on its effects. Such fixation, however, appears in the Freudian scheme to be a necessity, which must be acknowledged in order to modify it. The denial of it, the insistence upon a primal, unpopulated stage, freely capable of creation until constrained, would as such appear a narcissistic illusion (Chasseguet-Smirgel & Grunberger, 1986).

REFERENCES

Akhtar, S., & O'Neil, M. K. (Eds.) (2011). *On Freud's "Beyond the Pleasure Principle"*. London: Karnac.

Andreas-Salomé, L. (1921). The dual orientation of narcissism. S. A. Leavy (Trans.). Reprinted 1962 in *Psychoanalytic Quarterly, 31*: 1–30.

Anzieu, D. (1987). *Freud's Self-analysis*. P. Graham (Trans.). The International Psycho-Analytical Library, No. 118. Madison, CT: International Universities Press.

Apfelbaum, B. (1966). On ego psychology: A critique of the structural approach to psycho-analytic theory. *International Journal of Psychoanalysis, 47*: 451–475.

Baranger, W. (1991). Narcissism in Freud. In: J. Sandler, E. S. Person, & P. Fonagy (Ed.), *Freud's "On Narcissism: An Introduction"*. London: Yale University Press. [Reprinted London: Karnac, 2012.]

Borch-Jacobsen, M. (1988). *The Freudian Subject*. Redwood City, CA: Stanford University Press.

Borch-Jacobsen, M., & Shamdasani, S. (2012). *The Freud Files: An Inquiry into the History of Psychoanalysis*. New York: Cambridge University Press.

Bronfen, E. (1998). *The Knotted Subject: Hysteria and Its Discontents*. Princeton, NJ: Princeton University Press.

Butler, J. (1997). *The Psychic Life of Power*. Redwood City, CA: Stanford University Press.

Caropreso, F., & Simanke, R. T. (2008). Life and death in Freudian metapsychology: a reappraisal of the second instinctual dualism. In: S. Akhtar & M. K. O'Neil (Eds.), *On Freud's "Beyond the Pleasure Principle"*. London: Karnac, 2011.

Chasseguet-Smirgel, J., & Grunberger, B. (1986). *Freud or Reich? Psychoanalysis and illusion*. London: Free Association Books.

Cohen, J. (2007). "I-not-I": narcissism beyond the one and the other. In: A. Gaitanidis & P. Curk (Eds.), *Narcissism: A Critical Reader*. London: Karnac, e-book.

Copjec, J. (1994). *Read My Desire: Lacan against the Historicists*. London: MIT Press.

Deleuze, G. (1994). *Difference and Repetition*. New York: Bloomsbury.

Deleuze, G., & Guattari, F. (1977). *Anti-Oedipus—Capitalism and Schizophrenia*. New York: Viking.

Dufresne, T. (2000). *Tales from the Freudian Crypt: The Death Drive in Text and Context*. Redwood City, CA: Stanford University Press.

Egebak, N. (1980). *Psykoanalyse og videnskabsteori: Frem kapitler af en Freudlæsning*. Copenhagen: Berlingske Forlag.

Erikson, E. H. (1954). The dream specimen of psychoanalysis. *Journal of the American Psychoanalytic Association, 2*: 5–56.

Eysenck, H. (1985). *The Decline and Fall of the Freudian Empire*. London: Penguin.

Fayek, A. (1981). Narcissism and the death instinct. *International Journal of Psychoanalysis, 62*: 309–322.

Fayek, A. (2013). *Freud's Other Theory of Psychoanalysis—The Replacement of the Indelible Theory of Catharsis*. London: Jason Aronson.

Fayek, A. (2014). *Consciousness and the Aconscious in Psychoanalytic Theory*. London: Rowman & Littlefield.

Felman, S. (1993). *What Does a Woman Want?: Reading and Sexual Difference*. Baltimore, MD: Johns Hopkins University Press.

Fink, B. (1995). *The Lacanian Subject: Between Language and Jouissance*. Princeton, NJ: Princeton University Press.

Fink, B. (2004). *Lacan to the Letter: Reading Écrits Closely*. Minneapolis, MN: University of Minnesota Press.

Freud, A. (1936). *Jeg'et og Forsvarsmekanismerne*. London: Hogarth. [Reprinted 1984, Copenhagen: Hans Reitzels.]

Freud, S. (1888b). Hysteria. *S. E., 1*: 37–59. London: Hogarth.

Freud, S. (1889a). Review of August Forel's *Hypnotisme*. *S. E., 1*: 89–102. London: Hogarth.

Freud, S. (1892–93). A case of successful treatment by hypnotism. *S. E., 1*: 115–128. London: Hogarth.

Freud, S. (1894a). The neuro-psychoses of defence. *S. E., 3*: 41–61. London: Hogarth.

Freud, S. (1894a). Die Abwehr-Neuropsychosen. *G. W., 1*: 59–75. London: Imago.

Freud, S., with Breuer, J. (1895d). *Studies on Hysteria. S. E., 2*. London: Hogarth.

Freud, S. (1896a). Heredity and the aetiology of the neuroses. *S. E., 3*: 141–156. London: Hogarth.

Freud, S. (1896b). Further remarks on the neuro-psychoses of defence. *S. E., 3*: 157–185. London: Hogarth.

Freud, S. (1900a). *The Interpretation of Dreams. S. E., 4–5*. London: Hogarth.

Freud, S. (1900a). *Die Traumdeutung. G. W., 2–3*. London: Imago.

Freud, S. (1901b). *The Psychopathology of Everyday Life. S. E., 6*. London: Hogarth.

Freud, S. (1905c). *Jokes and Their Relation to the Unconscious. S. E., 8*. London: Hogarth.

Freud, S. (1905d). *Three Essays on the Theory of Sexuality. S. E., 7*: 123–246. London: Hogarth.

Freud, S. (1905d). *Drei Abhandlungen Zur Sexualtheorie. G. W., 5*: 29–163. London: Imago.

Freud, S. (1908b). Character and anal erotism. *S. E., 9*: 167–176. London: Hogarth.

Freud, S. (1908e). Creative writers and day-dreaming. *S. E., 9*: 141–154. London: Hogarth.

Freud, S. (1910i). The psycho-analytic view of psychogenic disturbance of vision. *S. E., 11*: 209–219. London: Hogarth.

Freud, S. (1910i). Die psychogene Sehstörung in psychoanalytischer Auffassung. *G. W., 8*: 94–104. London: Imago.

Freud, S. (1911b). Formulations on the two principles of mental functioning. *S. E., 12*: 213–226. London: Hogarth.

Freud, S. (1911c). Psycho-analytic notes on an autobiographical account of a case of paranoia (dementia paranoides). *S. E., 12*: 1–82. London: Hogarth.

Freud, S. (1914c). On narcissism: an introduction. *S. E., 14*: 67–102. London: Hogarth.

Freud, S. (1914c). Zur Einführung des Narzißmus. *G. W., 10*: 137–172. London: Imago.

Freud, S. (1915c). Instincts and their vicissitudes. *S. E., 14*: 109–140. London: Hogarth.

Freud, S. (1915c). Triebe und Triebschicksale. *G. W., 10*: 210–234. London: Imago.

Freud, S. (1915d). Repression. *S. E., 14*: 141–158. London: Hogarth.

Freud, S. (1915e). The unconscious. *S. E., 14*: 159–215. London: Hogarth.

Freud, S. (1915e). Das Unbewusste. *G. W., 10*: 264–306. London: Imago.

Freud, S. (1917a). A difficulty in the path of psycho-analysis. *S. E., 17*: 135–144. London: Hogarth.

Freud, S. (1917a). Eine Schwierigkeit der Psychoanalyse. *G. W.*, *12*: 3–15. London: Imago.

Freud, S. (1919e). "A Child Is Being Beaten": a contribution to the study of the origin of sexual perversions. *S. E.*, *17*: 175–204. London: Hogarth.

Freud, S. (1920g). *Beyond the Pleasure Principle*. *S. E.*, *18*: 1–64. London: Hogarth.

Freud, S. (1921c). *Group Psychology and the Analysis of the Ego*. *S. E.*, *18*: 65–144. London: Hogarth.

Freud, S. (1921c). *Massenpsychologie und Ich-Analyse*. *G. W.*, *13*: 73–165. London: Imago.

Freud, S. (1923b). *The Ego and the Id*. *S. E.*, *19*: 1–66. London: Hogarth.

Freud, S. (1923b). *Das Ich und das Es*. *G. W.*, *13*: 237–293. London: Imago.

Freud, S. (1926e). *The Question of Lay Analysis*. *S. E.*, *20*: 177–258. London: Hogarth.

Freud, S. (1933a). *New Introductory Lectures on Psycho-Analysis*. *S. E.*, *22*: 1–182. London: Hogarth.

Freud, S. (1933a). *Neue Folge der Vorlesungen zur Einführung in die Psychoanalyse*. *G. W.*, *15*. London: Imago.

Freud, S. (1950a). *The Origins of Psycho-Analysis*. *S. E.*, *1*: 175–399. London: Hogarth.

Freud, S. (1950c). Entwurf einer Psychologie. *G. W.*, *Nachtragsband*: 375–489. London: Imago.

Freud, S. (1954). *The Origins of Psychoanalysis: Letters, drafts and notes to Wilhelm Fliess (1887–1902)*. J. Strachey (Trans.). New York: Basic Books.

Freud, S. (1966). *The Standard Edition of the Complete Psychological Works of Sigmund Freud (S. E.)*. J. Strachey (Trans.). London: Hogarth.

Freud, S. (1980). *Udkast til en videnskabelig psykologi*. L. Andersen (Trans.). Copenhagen: Hans Reitzels.

Freud, S. (1991). *Gesammelte Werke (G. W.)*. A. Freud (Ed.). London: Imago.

Gaitanidis, A., & P. Curk (Ed.) (2007). *Narcissism: A Critical Reader*. London: Karnac, e-book.

Gammelgaard, J. (2016). Det ubevidste som et sprog: Jo vist—men hvilket sprog? *Lamella, tidsskrift for teoretisk psykoanalyse*, *1*: 173–186.

Gill, M., & Holtzman, P. S. (1976). Psychology versus metapsychology. *Psychological Issues*, Monograph 36, *9*(4). New York: International Universities Press.

Gill, M., & Pribram, K. H. (1976). *Freud's "Project" Reassessed: A Preface to Contemporary Cognitive Theory and Neuropsychology*. London: Hutchinson.

Green, A. (2001). *Life Narcissism, Death Narcissism*. London: Free Association Books.

Halperin, S., & Shakow, C. S. (1989). The development of identification in Freudian theory. *Psychoanalytic Review*, *76*: 353–374.

Hartmann, H. (1939). *Ego Psychology and the Problem of Adaptation*. New York: International Universities Press.

Hartmann, H. (1956). The development of the ego concept in Freud's work. *International Journal of Psychoanalysis*, 37: 425–438.

Hartmann, H., Kris, E., & Loewenstein, R. M. (1946). Comments on the formation of psychic structure. *Psychoanalytic Study of the Child*, 2: 11–38.

Hill, M. A. (1980). The concept of the ego and the schools of psychoanalysis. Ph.D. thesis, York University, UK.

Johnston, J. (2008). *The Allure of Machinic Life: Cybernetics, Artificial Life, and the New AI*. Cambridge, MA: MIT Press.

Jones, E. (1953). *The Life and Work of Sigmund Freud. Volume I*. New York: Basic Books.

Jones, E. (1955). *The Life and Work of Sigmund Freud. Volume II*. New York: Basic Books.

Kanzer, M. (1973). Two prevalent misconceptions about Freud's "Project" (1895). *Annual of Psychoanalysis*, 1: 88–103.

Karlsson, G. (1998). Beyond the pleasure principle: the affirmation of existence. *Scandinavian Psychoanalytic Review*, 21: 37–52.

Kojève, A. (1969). *Introduction to the Reading of Hegel*. Ithaca, NY: Cornell University Press, 1980.

Køppe, S., & Olsen, O. A. (1981). *Freuds psykoanalyse*. Copenhagen: Gyldendalske Boghandel, Nordisk.

Køppe, S., & Olsen, O. A. (1983). Introductions. *Sigmund Freud: Metapsykologi*. Copenhagen: Hans Reitzel.

Lacan, J. (1949). The mirror stage as formative of the I function. B. Fink (Trans.). In: *Écrits: The First Complete Edition in English*. New York: W. W. Norton, 2006.

Lacan, J. (1957). The instance of the letter in the unconscious: or reason since Freud. B. Fink (Trans.). In: *Écrits: The First Complete Edition in English*. New York: W. W. Norton, 2006.

Lacan, J. (1958). The direction of the treatment and the treatment and the principles of its power. B. Fink (Trans.). In: *Écrits: The First Complete Edition in English*. New York: W. W. Norton, 2006.

Lacan, J. (1977). *Seminar XI: The Four Fundamental Concepts of Psychoanalysis*. New York: W. W. Norton.

Lacan, J. (1988). *Seminar II: The Ego in Freud's Theory and in the Technique of Psychoanalysis, 1954–55*. New York: Cambridge University Press.

Lacan, J. (1991). *Seminar I: Freud's Papers on Technique, 1953–1954*. New York: W. W. Norton.

Laplanche, J. (1970). *Life and Death in Psychoanalysis*. London: Johns Hopkins University Press. [Reprinted Baltimore, MD: Johns Hopkins University Press, 1985.]

Laplanche, J. (1987). *Liv og død i psykoanalysen*. Aarhus, Denmark: KLIM.

Laplanche, J. (1999a). The so-called "death drive": sexual drive. In: R. Weatherhill (Ed.), *The Death Drive: New Life for a Dead Subject* (pp. 40–59). London. Rebus Press.

Laplanche, J. (1999b). *The Unconscious and the Id*. London: Rebus.

Laplanche, J. (2002/2003). Sublimation and/or inspiration. *New Formation*: 30–50.

Laplanche, J. (2004). The so-called "death drive": a sexual drive. *British Journal of Psychotherapy*, *20*: 455–471.

Laplanche, J. (2007). Closing and opening of the dream: Must chapter VII be rewritten? In: C. Liu, J. Mowitt, T. Pepper, & J. Spicer (Eds.), *The Dreams of Interpretation: A Century Down the Royal Road*. Minneapolis, MN: University of Minnesota Press.

Laplanche, J., & Pontalis, J.-B. (1973). *The Language of Psychoanalysis*. London: The International Psychoanalytical Library, Hogarth & Institute of Psychoanalysis.

Levin, K. (1978). *Freud's Early Psychology of the Neuroses: A Historical Perspective*. Hassocks, UK: Harvester Press.

Lind, L. (1991). Thanatos: the drive without a name: the development of the concept of the death drive in Freud's writings. *Scandinavian Psychoanalytic Review*, *14*: 60–80.

Lothane, Z. (1998). Freud's 1895 Project—from mind to brain and back again. *Annals of the New York Academy of Sciences*, *843*(1): 43–65.

Mansfield, N. (2000). *Subjectivity: Theories of the Self from Freud to Haraway*. New York: New York University Press.

Marcus, L. (Ed.) (1999). *Sigmund Freud's The Interpretation of Dreams: New Interdisciplinary Essays*. Manchester, UK: Manchester University Press.

Markotic, L. (2001). There where primary narcissism was, I must become: The inception of the ego in Andreas-Salomé, Lacan, and Kristeva. *American Imago*, *58*: 813–836.

McIntosh, D. (1986). The ego and the self in the thought of Sigmund Freud. *International Journal of Psychoanalysis*, *67*: 429–448.

Mehlman, J. (1976). Trimethylamin: Notes on Freud's specimen dream. *Diacritics*, *6*(1): 42–45.

Moncayo, R. (2008). *Evolving Lacanian Perspectives for Clinical Psychoanalysis: On Narcissism, Sexuation, and the Phases of Analysis in Contemporary Culture*. London: Karnac.

Montgomery, S. L. (2001). A case of (mis)taken identity? II: Freudian language in the ego and the id. *Psychoanalytic Review*, *88*: 51–81.

Nietzsche, F. (2001). *Nietzsche: Beyond Good and Evil: Prelude to a Philosophy of the Future (Cambridge Texts in the History of Philosophy)*. New York: Cambridge University Press.

Phillips, A. (1988). *Winnicott*. Glasgow, UK: William Collins, Sons.

Rabaté, J.-M. (2007). "In dreams begin responsibilities": toward dream ethics. In: C. Liu, J. Mowitt, T. Pepper, & J. Spicer (Eds.), *The Dreams of Interpretation: A Century Down the Royal Road*. Minneapolis, MN: University of Minnesota Press.

Rieff, P. (1979). *Freud: The Mind of the Moralist*. Chicago, IL: University of Chicago Press.

Rose, N. (1998). *Inventing Our Selves: Psychology, Power, and Personhood*. Cambridge: Cambridge University Press.

Rothstein, A. (1981). The ego: An evolving construct. *International Journal of Psychoanalysis, 62*: 435–445.

Schafer, R. (1976). *A New Language for Psychoanalysis*. New Haven, CT: Yale University Press.

Schmidt-Hellerau, C. (2001). *Life Drive & Death Drive: Libido and Lethe—a Formalized Consistent Model of Psychoanalytic Drive and Structure Theory*. New York: Other Press.

Tomlinson, C. W. (2011). *Jenseits* and beyond: teaching Freud's late work. In: S. Akhtar & M. K. O'Neil (Eds.), *On Freud's "Beyond the Pleasure Principle"*. London: Karnac.

Verhaeghe, P. (1999). *Does the Woman Exist? (revised ed.)*. New York: Other Press.

Weber, S. (1982). *The Legend of Freud*. Redwood City, CA: Stanford University Press.

Welsh, A. (1994). *Freud's Wishful Dream Book*. Woodstock, UK: Princeton University Press.

Wilson, E. (1996). Projects for a scientific psychology: Freud, Derrida, and connectionist theories of cognition. *Differences: A journal of feminist cultural studies, 8*(3): 21–52.

Yorke, C. (1991). Freud's "On narcissism"—a teaching text. In: J. Sandler, E. S. Person, & P. Fonagy (Eds.), *Freud's "On Narcissism: An Introduction"*. London: Yale University Press. [Reprinted London: Karnac, 2012.]

Yorke, C. (1994). Freud or Klein: Conflict or compromise. *International Journal of Psychoanalysis, 75*: 375–385.

Žižek, S. (2008). *Violence*. New York: Picador.

INDEX

Mansfield, N., xxi
Marcus, L., 30
Markotic, L., 47
masochism, 49
maturation of drives, 50–53
McIntosh, D., xxiii
Mehlman, J., 42
melancholia, 71
metaphoric scheme, xv–xvii, 48,
    57–66, 73–77, 81, 86
metapsychology vs metaphysics,
    xxiii
metonymic scheme, xv–xvii, 48–58,
    61–63, 65, 72–77, 81, 86
Moncayo, R., 47
monism, energetic, 56
Montgomery, S. L., 69, 71–72
moral cowardice, 8, 12
mother, 48, 53, 61, 77–79
mycelium, 40

nahestehende Fremde, 82
narcissism, xi, xv–xvii, xxiii, 47–48,
    53, 56–69, 71, 73–74, 77–78,
    81–83, 85–86, 88
navel of the dream, 40
needs, 11–12, 15, 31–32, 47–49, 51,
    53–54, 60, 64–66, 83, 86
neurological discourse in Freud, xiii,
    13–16
neuron doctrine, 10
neurones, types of, 10
neurosis, xiii, 2–3, 7–8, 11, 14, 28, 42
new psychic action, xvi, 59–61, 63
Nietzsche, F., 80

object choice, 64, 71, 77–79
obsessional neurosis, 28
oedipal/Oedipus, 61, 75, 77–79, 85,
    90
Olsen, O. A., xxiii, 26–27, 55–56, 70,
    72, 80

O'Neil, M. K., 80
ontogenesis, xxii, 47–48, 50, 58, 63,
    65, 86
oral, 78
organic, xvii, 23, 38, 48, 55, 60, 80–84
organism, xvi, xxii, 8, 11–12, 14, 16,
    21, 47–48, 53–54, 56, 65–66,
    77, 81–82, 86
Otto, dream of the sick, 36
ouroboros, 63
overdetermination, 15, 19, 27, 35,
    42, 74

paranoia, 59
parasite, 9
parents, 62–63, 78–79, 87
pathoanatomical model of neurosis,
    2–3
pathogenic idea, xii, 3–9
Pcpt., system, 24, 68, 70, 73
Pcs., system, 24–27, 30–31, 35, 42, 68,
    71, 74
perception, 31, 72
period of latency, 50
perversion, 50, 54, 57
phantasy, xx–xxi, 27–29, 75–76, 86
Phillips, A., xxii
Plato, 81, 87
pleasure principle, 11, 51, 53, 60, 79,
    82
Pontalis, J. -B., xxii, 34–35, 53, 56, 59,
    64, 70, 73, 82
post-structuralism, xix, xxi
preconscious, 30–31, 33, 39
predisposition, neurotic, 3
Pribram, K. H., 10, 13, 16
primal narcissism *see* primary
    narcissism
primary narcissism, xv, 53, 59–63
primary process, xiii–xiv, 10–12, 22,
    24–27, 82
principle of constancy, 11–12, 80, 82

For Product Safety Concerns and Information please contact our EU
representative GPSR@taylorandfrancis.com
Taylor & Francis Verlag GmbH, Kaufingerstraße 24, 80331 München, Germany